19.95

W9-ASP-278

Stangl POTTERY

An Ideal Day's Outing

A visit to the Stangl Pottery outlet makes an ideal day's outing. Bring a friend . . . or better yet, plan a trip with your church or social club. They'll love every minute of it.

If you're extra lucky, you'll get here during one of our occasional sales of Flemington Specials. These are special designs or items offered for a limited time only . . . priced so low you won't believe it.

The Pottery is easy to reach, and you can lunch in nearby Flemington. Everything's there, from hot dogs to delightful restaurants. Plan now to visit us soon.

We're open 10 to 5, every day of the year except Easter, Thanksgiving, Christmas, and New Year's . . . eager to welcome you!

How to Get There

FOLLOW THE GREEN ARROW
IN FLEMINGTON TO

STANGL POTTERY
Flemington, N. J.
Phone 201-782-2918

For Beautiful Bargains
In Dinnerware
and Giftware . . .

Stangl
POTTERY

Flemington, New Jersey

Stangl POTTERY

HARVEY DUKE

Wallace-Homestead Book Company
Radnor, Pennsylvania

Photo credits

Political mugs courtesy of Fred Israel, reprinted with permission of The Political Bandwagon, Box 348, Leola, PA 17540.

Rabbit pitcher, Della Ware Quimper bowl and Gingerbread dealer sign courtesy of Barbara Strauss.

Colonial relish photo by John Elder, courtesy of Johann, Chris and Steve McKee.

All other black and white photographs by David Pritchard, Grey Barn Photography, RD 1, Box 197, Belvidere, NJ 07823.

Cover photograph by Tom Dorshimer. Interior color by Mark Jenkins.

Opposite page: *The Apple Tree coaster adapted for use on Martin Stangl's farm in Hunterdon County.*

Copyright ©1993 by Harvey Duke
All Rights Reserved

Published in Radnor, Pennsylvania 19089, by Wallace Homestead,
a division of Chilton Book Company

No part of this book may be reproduced, transmitted, or stored
in any form or by any means, electronic or mechanical,
without prior written permission from the publisher

Designed by Anthony Jacobson
Manufactured in the United States of America

Library of Congress Cataloging-in-Publication Data

Duke, Harvey.
    Stangl Pottery / Harvey Duke.
        p. cm.
    Includes bibliographical references and index.
    ISBN 0-87069-674-2 (pbk.)
        1. Stangl Pottery Company--Catalogs. 2. Pottery, American--New
    Jersey--Trenton--Catalogs. I. Title.
    NK4210.S66A4 1993
    738'.09749'66--dc20   92-50192
                                                             CIP

2 3 4 5 6 7 8 9 0 1 2   3 2 1 0 9 8 7 6 5 4

To

Bob and Nancy Perzel
without whom this book would not exist

and to

Merrill and Christl Stangl Bacheler & Dave and Betty Stangl Thomas
and Kay Hackett and Anne Pogranicy
and especially Irene Sarnecki
who are still ardent Stangl employees
after all these years

Contents

Acknowledgments

Every book takes on its own personality, beyond an author's plans, shaped by the available material and the people who contribute to it. When I began interviews for Stangl Pottery, *I found myself with a growing treasury of anecdotal as well as factual material that had to be included, material that makes this book different from other books in the field.*

The people I am happy to thank are:

My friends David Caouette, Gus Gustafson, Jeff Nesler, Mickey and Gene Meier, and Pat Lyons, for carrying me through.

At my publisher, Chris Kuppig, General Manager, whose support of this book was very important to me; Susan Clarey, the tireless acquisitions editor, who worked so hard to see that this book was published; and Kathy Conover, my editor, who is a no-nonsense professional — the best you can ask for in an editor. And Harry Rinker, for being a good pal, always direct, truthful and wise.

Martin Stangl's daughters, Betty and her husband Dave Thomas, who was General Manager, and Christl and her husband Merrill Bacheler, who was Flemington Manager. Their graciousness in sharing memories of family and work was invaluable.

Stangl employees Edward Alvater, Kay Kastner Hackett, James Paul, Anne Pogranicy and Irene Los (Leash) Sarnecki and her husband Tom. All of these people welcomed me and were generous with their information and recollections. From my dealings with them, I can understand why everyone recalls working at Stangl so positively.

Dave Pritchard, my black-and-white photographer, for his patience and skill. And Mark Jenkins, our color photographer, for his equanimity and contributions.

I've always considered pottery collectors to be special people, and my experience with Stangl collectors has only increased my appreciation. There are not only those I contacted for the book, but those who called and offered pieces when word of the book got around. They shared not only their collections but their thoughts and collecting experience. Much of the wisdom in this book comes from them:

Muriel Brannon; Mary Jane Cassatt; Scott Creighton; Jim Davidson; Rhoda and Harold Dilts; Nancy Fisher who, besides lending objects to be photographed, acted as courier for others; Bobbie Garvey; Michael Gehl and Jeff Caruso; Jeannine Coup, editor of The Political Bandwagon; Skip and Dolores Hagar; Joan and Ed Hawley; Fred Israel; Dave and Doris Kerper, who went out of their way to make sure that every known bird was pictured; Mary McGreevy; Johann and Chris McKee; Steve McKee; Marjorie "The Stangl Lady" Moll; Terry Noll; Marty Parcel; Alton Parker; James Paul; Chester Piell; Bud Pyatt; Tom Rago, who specializes in Stangl and other Trenton potteries at the Main Street Antiques Center in Flemington; Miriam and George Rosenwasser; Barbara Strauss; Ed Stump of Raccoon's Tail Antiques in Mullica Hill, N.J.; and Richard Trickett.

For their hospitality and photographic support, my thanks to Luke and Nancy Ruepp for their insights, and for lending much of their Kiddie Ware and Country Life collections; and to Wayne and Diana Weigand, for sharing the wisdom of their experience, and for packing, unpacking and repacking over 100 birds for the photo session. Their enthusiasm helped sustain me when the going got tough. And both collections still dazzle my mind's eye.

Rob Runge for the long hours he gave and for his thoughtful insights, as well as much of the pottery pictured.

Last and most important, Bob and Nancy Perzel of Popkorn Antiques, wonderful friends, loving and giving, as well as impeccable dealers, whose love of Stangl inspired this book. Not only did they encourage me to write this from the start, they housed, fed and transported me during the time of my research and interviews, did all the scut work during tedious days of photography, and shared their collection and knowledge gained over almost twenty years of buying and selling Stangl. Miraculously, they stayed cheerful throughout. They are irreplaceable.

Consultants

General Consultant
Bob and Nancy Perzel
c/o Popkorn Antiques
4 Mine Street
Flemington, NJ 08822

Kiddie Ware, Country Life
Luke and Nancy Ruepp
PO Box 349
Lake Hiawatha, NJ 07034

Birds
Diana Weigand
325 West Upper Ferry Road, Apt C-2
Trenton, NJ 08628

Wayne Weigand
173 Pennsbury Plaza Boulevard
Morrisville, PA 19067

If you have specific questions, please write to my consultants. I will only be passing your letters on to them, so this will save you time. If you have any items that should be added to the listings, please write to me at: 115 Montague Street, Brooklyn, New York 11201. When writing to any of us, please type or clearly print your letter, try not to exceed one page, and enclose a self-addressed, stamped envelope if you wish a reply. Please keep questions to a minimum — two or three at the most, and make them specific. Any question requiring a long answer — such as "Tell me all you know about Stangl" — is unfair. Remember, the consultants answer questions as a courtesy.

Keep in mind that a sketch is better than a description, and a photo is better than a sketch. Please do not ask anyone to price unlisted items.

Preface

I was fortunate to find that many of the people who made Stangl the great pottery it was, were still available for interviews and research. Their words and memories are scattered through the book.

The pioneering work on collectible Stangl was in the books of Norma Rehl, published in 1979 and 1982. Since then, interest has grown, new items have turned up and, most important, much new information has surfaced. My publisher and I are happy to present the most thorough book on Stangl to date.

Stangl is almost unique, in that it is part of a tradition that had two flowerings, first as Fulper, then as Stangl. The cable that binds the two is Martin Stangl. He had a strong personality, was adventurous in his artistic exploration and astute in his marketing sense, yet parsimonious with his praise and not so willing to explore technological advances. It is telling that the company did not survive his death by more than a few years.

What I have come to understand from my research is that no book, no matter how big, can encompass all that was Stangl, for several reasons. Whereas most potteries generally destroyed their experimental pieces, everything that Stangl attempted was sold to the public through its outlet shop in Flemington. Also, Stangl used the Flemington outlet to "test market" new products. The experimental pieces were never documented; the test pieces may have been, but many records were lost in the fire of 1965.

Add to this the fact that many seconds were given unusual treatments and sold in Flemington. And during the summer, when department store trade was slow, lots of special items were made up and sent down to Flemington where tourist business was brisk.

This means that we can find hundreds of different items for which no documentation exists.

To further confuse things, Martin Stangl often rummaged among old molds for items to use in current lines. Irene Sarnecki: "He used to go up to the attic and resurrect things. He'd go through some of these [catalog pages]. He'd sit down, 'Irene, let's go through and see what we're going to have for the new art ware line this year.' [He'd say] 'We'll do this, we're not doing this.' He would cross things off, 'Yeah, we'll try this, we'll try that.' Basically, it got to the point where he could just go back to 1935, '36 or '37 and make a different line out of it."

All this means that you can find pieces of Stangl that no one else has, and for which there is no specific explanation. Given this wide panorama, what I have chosen to cover in the space I have are all the popular lines. I hope, naturally, that there will be a second edition with more space in which I can address some of the more singular pieces.

How to Use This Book

QUOTED MATERIAL Material in quotation marks, if not attributed to an interview, is from company literature. In quoted material, certain words have been added in square brackets to clarify the text or indicate editing.

PATTERN NAMES Whenever possible, Stangl's names have been used. Stangl was better than many potteries when it came to putting pattern names on the back of ware. However, if no Stangl name existed, I did one of two things: 1. used the name that collectors have adopted; or, 2. made up a name (both are in quotation marks). It's important to have names for everything, to facilitate buying and selling by mail.

NUMBERING AND DATING A number following a slash mark, found after a shape name, is the equivalent shape number; a slash and a number found after a decoration name is the equivalent decoration number. I've included them to help you make a more positive identification where possible.

Dates of introduction, when known, are in parentheses. If there is some question, "ca" will be used; "<" means at least the year indicated, possibly earlier.

COLORS AND SIZES When possible, I have included colors listed in the catalogs, as well as colors found by collectors. Other colors can turn up.

Because of the nature of the manufacturing process, sizes will differ somewhat from the measurements given; the larger the piece, the more variance possible.

A WORD ON ORGANIZATION When you're dealing with a pottery whose product is as diverse as Stangl's, the material could be presented in a number of ways. I have arranged them alphabetically by the most obviously logical category, but you will find a number of cross-references throughout the text that will enable you to locate additional information on some pieces or lines.

TERMINOLOGY Much of what Stangl made, aside from the dinnerware, can be classified as *artware* or *giftware*. Artware because of the style and handwork, giftware because that is how it was meant to be sold. Stangl used both terms.

The carving process used by Stangl is generally known as *sgraffito,* especially in reference to the Pennsylvania Dutch ware that was an inspiration for this line; but Stangl called the process "carving" and the employees who did the work were referred to as carvers, so I have used this term throughout. Some items were never carved and, where listed, have "(nc)" after them.

I've used Stangl's terminology for some items: *Flower Pot* for planter, and *Flower Block* or *Insert* for flower frog. What many collectors call the skillet or frypan casserole was called *casserole with handle* by Stangl.

PRICING I have used either a single price or a range, depending on what is appropriate to the item. Prices for items that are worth at least a certain amount, but for which it is a seller's market, are indicated by a plus sign after the base price, *e.g.,* $500 + . One of a kind, or nearly so, items are marked ND for "Not Determined." This does not mean the sky is the limit on prices for these items; desirability plays an important part in valuing a piece. Prices are for items in mint condition.

People who still want to buy cheaply may be disappointed, thinking my prices high, and some sellers will complain they are too low. That's par for the course. I have worked hard to make sure these prices are as real as they can be, reflecting the market, not leading or following it. Because most of the buying and selling of Stangl takes place in the northeast, where it was manufactured, I have used that area as the base of my pricing, as I believe it to be the most accurate.

Finally, I close with the standard phrase, though many people believe it falls on deaf ears: these prices are meant to be a guide, not a bible.

History

The information in this section has been taken from company records and literature, as well as interviews, except where otherwise indicated.

There is some question about the date Fulper/Stangl started in business. All Stangl literature gives 1805 as the year the company began. However, Paul Evans, in his thoroughly researched book *Art Pottery of the United States* (see Bibliography) has the following to say: "The operation which was to become the Fulper Pottery was established in 1814 at the corner of Mine and Main Streets, Flemington by Samuel Hill."

Samuel Hill was drawn to Hunterdon County by the presence of good beds of red burning clays. He began by manufacturing drain tiles, always needed by farmers. Success led him to introduce other rough-cast items, such as bowls and drinking foundations for poultry.

Samuel Hill died in 1858. The plant was purchased by Abraham Fulper, a nephew who worked for him. Evans gives the date of purchase as 1860, but suggests Fulper may have been renting the pottery as of 1857.

Under Abraham, who died in 1881, and his three sons, Edward, George W. and William, the business expanded to include water and vinegar jugs, pickling jars, butter churns, ginger beer bottles and mugs. One important item was the Fulper Germ Proof Filter, stoneware jars set together to provide cool, clear water. This was a popular item in railroad stations and other public waiting rooms in both the northern and southern hemisphere. Much of this stoneware was decorated or labeled in cobalt blue, a color favored by potters because varying kiln temperatures never affected the color.

The company name changed a few times (G. W. Fulper & Bros. and Fulper Bros.) but was incorporated in 1899 as the Fulper Pottery Company. The company introduced Vasekraft art pottery line in 1909, though Evans notes that experimental production was probably carried on from 1906. Many of the glazes and designs were developed by William H. Fulper II, president.

Company history gives 1910 as the year that Johann Martin Stangl, born in Hof, Germany, July 30, 1888, began his employ with the company. A student of design and ceramic engineering at the industrial school in Bunzlau, Germany, Stangl was hired as chemist and plant superintendent. Evans notes that Stangl's name first appears in the members' directory of The American Ceramic Society Transactions in 1911, where he is listed as the superintendent of the technical division of Fulper. Stangl left Fulper in 1914 to develop an industrial art ware line for the Haeger Potteries of Dundee, Illinois. He returned to Fulper in 1920 as general manager.

In 1924, the "Fulper Fayence" colors of Chinese Ivory, Colonial Blue, Silver Green and Persian Yellow were introduced: "Exceptional in Merit—Utmost in Value." The 1924 catalog is the earliest one I have seen, and it pictures a tea set and luncheon set, shape #901, in these colors. This predates the introduction of solid colors on California dinnerware, and would seem to answer the question of which was the first pottery to market such ware.

It is said that these sets were devised by Martin Stangl to bolster the sagging fortunes of the Fulper Pottery and that William Fulper did not like them. So, in 1926, the Anchor Pottery in Trenton, New Jersey, was purchased. It had been owned by the Grand Union Tea Company and used to manufacture premiums that Grand Union gave away in its house-to-house sales programs. Here, far away from Flemington, these sets could be made out of Fulper's sight. Low cost art wares were also added to the line.

In 1928 William Fulper died. Information is unclear, but it would seem that Martin Stangl became president in 1928, and two years later bought the company.

The decade of the twenties was pivotal: from the production of art pottery, some expensive, some more affordable, at the beginning of the decade, to the production of dinnerware, low cost art ware and utilitarian ware at the end. This was no doubt due in part to declining interest in art pottery, but there must have been other factors. Undoubtedly, Martin Stangl's ideas about where he wanted to take the company were one of them.

In 1929 the plant in Flemington burned down, leaving only the kiln. It was a terrible fire with sparks flying and members of the Fulper family, who lived next door to the pottery, moved their furniture one house down because they feared their house would burn. It did not.

All manufacturing was temporarily concentrated in Trenton while work began in Flemington. Rather than rebuild the original factory, Stangl decided to enlarge a building just down Mine Street that had originally been an ice cream factory. At the time of the fire it was being used for storage of clay and other material. This building was expanded, kilns added, then a showroom introduced. Though some manufacturing was brought back to Flemington for a while, soon it was all concentrated in Trenton, while the kilns in Flemington were used for demonstrations.

In 1940 Stangl became the first pottery in America to manufacture bird figures in pottery and, in 1942, in porcelain. They precede Boehm and Cybis, other famous bird producers, by a decade.

In 1942 Stangl brought out its unique hand-carved, hand-painted dinnerware on a red body, which was a bestseller until the factory closed. The red body would be used exclusively for the dinnerware and art wares, the white body which had been used for all the lines was retained for the birds.

There has been some question as to when the name was officially changed from Fulper to Stangl. Many advertisements from the thirties use both names, announcing new Stangl Pottery lines, with the Fulper Pottery name and address at the foot of the advertisement. Company records show 1955 as the correct date.

In 1956 Stangl bought two gold kilns — kilns that could be fired at the proper temperature for gold and decals. This capability allowed experimentation with gold and silver decoration; Stangl devised the dry-brushed artware lines. At the same time, it experimented with a china body, used for the Christmas decal items, and a few other things.

On August 25, 1965, there was a fire in the Trenton plant due to the aged wiring. Approximately half of the building, including materials and records, was destroyed: the offices, warehouse and decorating department. The kilns and machinery were unaffected. A temporary decorating department was set up and production resumed in about two weeks. The damaged section was rebuilt and staff moved back on May 17, 1966. Immediately after the fire, only the white body was made. The red body was re-introduced some months later but did not totally replace the white body. The red body would be discontinued in October of 1974.

Martin Stangl was hospitalized with a heart attack on October 18, 1971. He died on February 13, 1972. His estate ran the pottery until it was purchased by Frank Wheaton, Jr., of Wheaton Industries, Millville, N.J., on June 27, 1972; production of Stangl pottery continued. However, on July 23, 1978, Wheaton sold all assets to the Pfaltzgraff Pottery Company, a division of Susquehanna Broadcasting, and production ceased. Remaining office staff was gradually laid off, and Stangl officially closed on November 1, 1978. Pfaltzgraff bought Stangl for the real estate, specifically the outlet shop in Flemington which, as of this writing, is a Pfaltzgraff outlet shop.

Marks

IMPRESSED Many Stangl items (the dinnerware is a major exception) have an impressed mark (these are in the molds) containing either "Stangl" or "Stangl USA" and the shape number. Some pieces are too small for all three and may only have a number. Sometimes these are not easy to read because they are filled in with glaze or the mold has become worn (molds were replaced periodically because they lost their crispness with use). Rarely, "TR" will be found impressed on the bottom of a piece of Terra Rose.

HAND-PAINTED Beginning with the hand-painted dinnerware of the late thirties, the name or initial of the decorator was painted on the bottom of the piece (names are found more readily on the late thirties' white-bodied dinnerware, initials on the red-bodied dinnerware and the birds). Because many decorators had the same name, some are actual initials, some are code. Unlike many other potteries, the decorators at Stangl painted the entire piece, rather than doing one element and passing it along to others to finish. A second set of incised initials may often be found; these belong to the carver.

Please do not confuse these with artist-signed pieces that other potteries produced. The decorators were artisans, not artists, and had varying degrees of skill. Their initials are on these pieces not because of pride of work (though I am sure there was that) but for reasons of quality control.

STAMPED The hand-painted square, oval, Terra Rose and bird marks are all rubber stamped, usually under the glaze. The oval

Two versions of the early square-stamped mark, the bottom one used for hand-painted ware.

stamp often contains the name of the pattern or finish. You can date pieces made from 1951 onward because in that year Stangl began adding roman numerals to the oval mark. So an oval with three numerals means 1953. After 1960 (represented by an X), slashes were made in the rim of the oval to indicate years. This saved money on new rubber stamps.

SECONDS Stangl did not mark its seconds until the dinnerware lines were introduced in the forties. Kay Hackett: "Then after a period of time it became necessary to mark all the seconds. They sand-blasted them with pecan shells, I think. A little [oval] with a little Stangl in it, because people were buying things in Flemington and taking them into New York [stores] and saying, 'This is defective. Give me a good one.' So that was when that became necessary." This mark looks white on many pieces, but sometimes you need to catch the light in just the right way in order to see it. Another seconds mark is a stamped "Stangl" in an oval, occasionally found with "Sec."

The oval stamp showing the roman numeral VIII, indicating this piece was made in 1958.

The basic stamped oval mark.

The version of the stamped oval mark used on hand-painted items, in this example showing the pattern name and the decorator's initials. Stangl was constantly changing and improving its body, and in later years "Oven Proof" was added to the mark.

The stamped mark used on Terra Rose.

Two versions of the seconds stamp.

The stamped mark used on the pottery birds. A different mark was used for the porcelain birds.

BIRDS OF AMERICA

The bird series was sold in the better gift and jewelry shops and department stores around the country.

In 1940 Stangl introduced a line of pottery birds which it expanded greatly in 1942 when WWII cut off Japanese imports. The return of foreign competition in 1947 resulted in curtailed production, with sporadic reissues until 1977. Birds continued in production until 1978. These later birds are dated.

Many of the birds were designed by Auguste Jacob after Audubon prints, some replicating the exact Audubon poses. (The valuable Audubon bird book was never left lying around at the pottery; it was kept in the safe.) If you look carefully, you can see Jacob's last name impressed at the very bottom of the large Cockatoo, slightly left of front. For this reason, some collectors refer to it as Jacob's Cockatoo. Some birds marked "Fulper," with glass eyes, that would seem to predate this line, have been found. They strongly resemble some of the birds listed here but have different numbers. There is a good chance they were designed by Jacob as well.

Stangl birds will be found in a white body with the exception of the terra cotta birds listed below. Stangl did not number consistently; the gaps in numbers do not signify birds yet to be discovered.

Porcelain Edition

Stangl made an early limited edition of twelve birds in porcelain (1942). They differ markedly from the pottery birds in that the porcelain ones have much more elaborate decoration, more leaves and flowers. A porcelain body allows for finer detail than a pottery body.

The porcelain birds were decorated in an area separate from the pottery birds. Irene Sarnecki: "We had a huge room where we had all of our dinnerware on display, the wall must have run about 75 feet, it was like bookcases, and there was one section, only [a few people] knew where it was, it would open up, and you'd go into that room and the room was left [exactly as] the day they stopped painting the porcelain birds. I guess they weren't going over too well 'cause they were considerably more expensive than the others. Everything was left, it was just like a museum. It would give you an eerie feeling, the brushes and the paint, you could see where the water was in the bowl that had dried out. It was just birds all over the place, and then we had the fire and that was the end of that entire building section. It was like a museum and it burned.

"There were only so many [sets made] and how many actually were sold, there might have been a hundred sets but I remember this room and I would say if there are fifty sets out, you're lucky. Because the place still had all these birds, and I would say, at the most, if there were fifty out there someplace, that is a lot." Some collectors feel that an estimate of a dozen sets sold might even be high.

Pricing. These birds were expensive when they were introduced; original prices are given in parentheses. It is a seller's market on these very rare birds.

3725	Red-headed Woodpecker ($60)	ND
3726	Crossbill ($50)	ND
3727	Crossbill, pair ($125)	ND
3728	Scissor-tailed Flycatcher ($150)	ND
3729	Red-headed Woodpecker, pair ($125)	ND
3738	Magpie–Jay ($175)	ND
3739	Audubon Warbler ($35)	ND
3740	Audubon Warbler, pair ($75)	ND
3741	Robin ($150)	ND
3742	Robin, pair ($250)	ND
3749	Scarlet Tanager ($50)	ND
3750	Scarlet Tanager, pair ($100)	ND

Pottery Series

There will be some variation in coloring and quality because these birds were painted by dozens of different decorators. In fact, demand was so great in the forties, with space limited in the decorating department in Trenton, that people were hired to work from their homes. In order to make sure that the paint wouldn't run while the decorated birds were being transported back to the factory to be fired, molasses was mixed with the colors. It burned away in the firing.

A number of the birds had more elaborate decoration than others, with leaves and flowers that were both made and applied by hand. They were among the first to be discontinued when demand slowed, because of the amount of labor involved and because many experienced workers went to work in defense plants during the war. When birds were first introduced, there were about fifty decorators (in-factory and at home); by the end of the decade there were fifteen.

Some birds with markedly different coloring will turn up. These are either color variations done deliberately by Stangl, which are noted in my listings, or are oddities that may be: (1) experimental colors; or (2) done by decorators for themselves. I indicate the latter with an asterisk in the price column. The Antique Ivory and Turquoise Blue Crackled pieces were dipped in tea to achieve the desired effect.

Those birds, such as the Cardinal and the Scarlet Tanager, which take an overglaze red, will sometimes be found with just white bodies and decorated head and base. These are seconds that had some imperfection and were not sent on for the final overglaze red. They were sent to Flemington, however, to be sold; Stangl never threw anything away. Because these were glazed prior to the red being applied, collectors finding them mistakenly think they are finished birds. Also, if you find a bird with a matte finish instead of the usual high gloss, it is one that was not sprayed heavily enough with glaze. It should have been touched up at the factory, but was not.

A single White Headed Pigeon is talked about but has never been seen. It may be that the single is presumed to exist because there is a double. The Broadtail Humming Bird and the Rivoli Humming Bird are the same figure, but with different numbers and different colored flower. The white birds were made in the 1970s for Royal Cumberland by Royal Dorchester, a subsidiary of Wheaton Industries, using the original Stangl molds. A number of birds have also been found as lamp bases.

Be alert for repairs. Many figures have been restored with varying degrees of skill, some so well that even a scrupulous dealer can be fooled. Because of the intricacy of some of these figures, examine them very carefully.

If one measurement is given, it is for height; two measurements are for height x length. Most measurements are from catalog sheets; actual sizes may vary a little. All spellings are per Stangl's catalogs. Variations in names are indicated in parentheses. If one Terra Rose color has been found, we could assume that all three were made; however, I have listed only those that have been confirmed.

See also *Animals* for information about an unusual duck.

3250 A–F: Standing Duck, Preening Duck, Feeding Duck, Gazing Duck, Drinking Duck, Quacking Duck.

Pricing. Prices are for the natural colors; alternate colors are priced separately below each entry. A slash (/) means "or" as in "Greenish/Tan" means the price is for greenish or tan.

3250 A	Standing Duck, 3¼″	60–75
	Antique/Black/Granada	
	Gold/Green Lustre/Platina/	
	Terra Rose Blue/Green/	
	Mauve	60–75
	White	5
3250 B	Preening Duck, 2¾″	60–75
	Antique/Black/Granada	
	Gold/Green Lustre/Platina/	
	Terra Rose Blue/Green/	
	Mauve	60–75
	White	5
3250 C	Feeding Duck, 1¾″	60–75
	Antique/Black/Granada	
	Gold/Green Lustre/	
	Platina/Terra Rose	
	Blue/Green/Mauve	60–75
	White	5
3250 D	Gazing Duck, 3¾″	60–75
	Antique/Black/Granada	
	Gold/Green Lustre/Platina/	
	Terra Rose Blue/Green/	
	Mauve	60–75
	White	5
3250 E	Drinking Duck, 1½″	60–75
	Antique/Black/Granada	
	Gold/Green Lustre/Platina/	
	Terra Rose Blue/Green/	
	Mauve	60–75
	White	5
3250 F	Quacking Duck, 3¼″	60–75
	Antique/Black/Granada	
	Gold/Green Lustre/Platina/	
	Terra Rose Blue/Green/	
	Mauve	60–75
	White	5
3273	Rooster, 5¾″	ND
	Antique Ivory Crackled/	
	Turquoise Blue Crackled	ND
3274	Penguin, 6″	400
	Antique Ivory Crackled/	
	Turquoise Blue Crackled	ND
	Terra Rose Mauve	ND

3433/16″ Rooster

3273/5¾″ Rooster

3430/22" Duck: Only two have been reported; one is marked "Fulper" and the other, shown here, was bisque fired in 1940. In an unglazed state, it was the decorating room mascot until it was glazed and fired in 1978. It was the last piece to go through the kiln when Stangl closed.

An unlisted White Wing Crossbill group. It may have been made up as a sample and never produced; this is the only one known.

3275	Turkey, 3½″	400–450
	Greenish/Tan	400–450
3276 S	Bluebird, 5″	80–100
	Antique Ivory Crackled/	
	Turquoise Blue Crackled	ND
3276 D	Bluebirds, pair, 8½″	150–170
3285	Rooster, 4½″	
	Early/Late	40–50
3285	Rooster, shaker	
	Early/Late	40–50
3286	Hen, 3¼″	
	Early/Late	40–50
3286	Hen, shaker	
	Early/Late	40–50

[Early hen and rooster had blue-green base w/ black decoration on feathers. Late version had lime green base w/ white bodies.]

3400	Love Bird, single, 4″	40–60
	Antique Ivory Crackled/	
	Turquoise Blue Crackled	ND
	Terra Rose mauve	ND
3400	Love Bird, single, revised, 4″	40–60
3401 S	Wren, tan (light brown), 3½″	50–60
3401 S	Wren, revised, dark brown, 3½″	35–50
	Antique/Black/Granada Gold	25–35

3401 D	Wren, pair, tan (light brown), 8″	125–150
3401 D	Wren, pair, revised, dark brown, 8″	70–90
3402 S	Oriole, beak down, 3¼″	100–150
	Antique Ivory Crackled	ND
	Terra Rose green/mauve	ND
3402 S	Oriole, revised, 3¼″	50–65
	Antique/Black/Granada Gold	ND
	Antique Ivory Crackled	ND
3402 D	Oriole, pair, 5½″	100–125
3402 D	Oriole, pair, revised, w/leaves, 5½″	100–125
3404 D	Love Birds, pair, kissing, 4½″	100–125
3404 D	Love Birds, pair, revised, not kissing, 5½″	100–125
3405 S	Cockatoo, 6″	50–65
	Antique Ivory Crackled/	
	Turquoise Blue Crackled	ND
	White	ND
3405 D	Cockatoo, pair, 9½″	110–135
	Antique Ivory Crackled	110–135
	White	110–135
3405 D	Cockatoo, pair, revised, open base, 9½″	100–125
3406 S	Kingfisher, 3½″	50–75
	Black	*

	Antique Ivory Crackled/	
	Turquoise Blue Crackled	50–75
	Terra Rose blue	50–75
3406 D	Kingfisher, pair, 5"	100–125
	Turquoise Blue Crackled	100–125
3407	Owl, 4"	275–325
	Turquoise Blue Crackled	275–325
3408	Bird of Paradise, 5½"	80–100
3430	Duck, 22"	ND
3431	Duck, standing, 8"	300–400
3432	Duck, running, 5"	
	Brown/Grayish white w/black	
	spots	300–400
	Marbleized	ND
3433	Rooster, 16"	ND
	Gray/Green	ND
3443	Flying Duck, 9"	250–275
	Antique Gold/Platina	250–275

[Basically gray, you will find variations in blue or green shading on the wings.]

3444	Cardinal, pine cones, (female)	
	6½"	80–90
3444	Cardinal, revised, 7"	
	Pink glossy	75–80
	Red matte	90–110
3445	Rooster, gray/yellow, 9"	125–150
	Antique Gold/Platina	125–150
3446	Hen, gray/yellow, 7"	125–150
	Antique Gold/Platina	125–150

[For the above two birds, shades of gray vary from light to dark; brown highlights on the yellow will vary in intensity as well.]

3447	Yellow (Prothonatary) Warbler,	
	5"	65–75
3448	Blue-headed Vireo, 4¼"	60–70
3449	Paroquet (Parrot), 5½"	75–150
3450	Passenger Pigeon, 9" x 18"	500+
3451	Willow Ptarmigan, 11" x 11"	800
3452	Painted Bunting, 5"	80–100
3453	Mountain Bluebird, 6⅛"	450–550
3454	Key West Quail Dove, 9"	250–325
3454	Key West Quail Dove, wings	
	spread	ND
	White	ND
3455	Shoveler, 12¼" x 14"	900–1000
3456	Cerulean Warbler, 4¼"	55–65
3457	Pheasant, 7¼" x 15"	ND

3458	Quail, 7½"	1000–1100
3459	Fish Hawk (Falcon/Osprey), 9½"	2000+
3490 D	Redstarts, pair, 9"	150–175
3491	Hen Pheasant, 6¼" x 11"	175–200
	Antique Gold/Platina	175–200
3492	Cock Pheasant, 6¼" x 11"	175–200
	Antique Gold/Platina	175–200
3518 D	White Headed Pigeon, pair,	
	7½" x 12½"	500–600
3580	Cockatoo, medium, 8⅞"	80–100
	Ivory matte w/pale yellow comb	110–140
3581	Chickadees, group (three),	
	5½" x 8½"	150–200
3582	Parrakeets, pair, blue/green, 7"	175–200
3583	Parula Warbler, 4¼"	40–65
3584	Cockatoo, large, 11⅜"	175–225
	Antique Gold/Platina	100–125
	Ivory matte w/pale green comb	250–300
3585	Rufous Humming Bird, 3"	40–65
	Antique Gold/Platina	40–65
3586	Pheasant, 9" x 15½"	450
	Terra Rose green/mauve,	
	9" x 16¼"	450
3589	Indigo Bunting, 3¼"	55–70
3590	Chat (Carolina Wren), 4½"	100–150
3591	Brewer's Blackbird, 3½"	80–100
3592	Titmouse, 2½"	50–60
	Blue glossy/Blue matte	ND
	White	ND
3593	Nuthatch, 2½"	50–60
3594	Red-faced Warbler, 3"	60–75
3595	Bobolink, 4¾"	100–125
3596	Gray Cardinal (Pyrrhuloxia), 4¾"	70–80
3597	Wilson Warbler, 3½"	40–60
3598	Kentucky Warbler, 3"	40–60
	Antique/Granada Gold/Platina	40–60
3599	Humming Birds, pair, 8" x 10½"	175–250
3625	Bird of Paradise, 13½"	1000+
3626	Broadtail Humming Bird, blue	
	flower, 6"	100–125
3627	Rivoli Humming Bird, pink	
	flower, 6"	100–125
3628	Rieffers Humming Bird, 4½"	100–125
3629	Broadbill Humming Bird, 4½"	100–125
3634	Allen Humming Bird, 3½"	60–75
3635	Goldfinches, group (four),	
	4" x 11½"	200
	White with black	*

Allen Humming Bird/3634

Audubon Warbler/3755S

Audubon Warbler,
pair/3756D

Bird of Paradise/3625

Bird of Paradise/3408

Blackpoll Warbler/3810

Black-throated Green
Warbler/3814

Blue Jay (peanut)/3715

Blue Jay (leaf)/3716

Blue Jay, pair/3717

Bluebird/3276S

Bluebirds, pair/3276D

Blue-headed
Vireo/3448

Bobolink/3595

Brewer's
Blackbird/3591

Broadbill Humming
Bird/3629

Broadtail Humming Bird,
blue flower/3626

Canary left, blue
flower/3747

Canary right, rose
flower/3746

Cardinal/3444

Pine cones   revised
(also *Female*)

Cerulean Warbler/3456

Chat (Carolina
Wren)/3590

Chestnut-backed
Chickadee/3811

Chestnut-sided
Warbler/3812

Chickadees, group (three)/3581

Cliff Swallow/3852

Cockatoo, small/3405S

Cockatoo, medium/3580

Cockatoo, large/3584

Cockatoo, pair/3405D

Cockatoo, pair,
revised, open
base/3405D

Duck, running/3432

Duck, flying/3443

Duck, standing/3431

European Finch/3722

Evening Grosbeak/3813

Fish Hawk
(Falcon/Osprey)/3459

Golden-crowned
Kinglet/3848

Golden-Crowned Kinglets,
group/3853

Goldfinch/3849

Goldfinches, group/3635

Gray Cardinal
(Pyrrhuloxia)/3596

Hen/3286

Hen/3446

Humming Birds, pair/3599

Indigo Bunting/3589

Kentucky Warbler/3598

Key West Quail Dove/3454

Kingfisher/3406S

Kingfisher, pair/3406D

Love Bird, single/3400
old   revised

Love Birds, pair/3404D
old, kissing   revised, not kissing

Magnolia Warbler/3925

Magpie-Jay/3758

Mountain Bluebird/3453

Nuthatch/3593

Oriole/3402S
old, beak down   revised

Oriole, pair/3402D
old   revised, w/leaves

Owl/3407

Painted Bunting/3452

Paroquet (Parrot)/3449

Parrakeets, pair/3582

Parula Warbler/3583

Passenger Pigeon/3450

Penguin/3274

Pheasant, Cock/3492

Pheasant, Hen/3491

Pheasant/3586 (Della Ware)

Pheasant/3457

Quail/3458

Red-breasted
Nuthatch/3851

Red-faced
Warbler/3594

Red-Headed
Woodpecker/3751

Red-Headed Woodpecker, pair/3752D

Redstarts, pair/3490D

Rieffers Humming Bird/3628

Rivoli Humming Bird, pink flower/3627

Rooster/3285

Rooster/3445

Rufous Humming Bird/3585

Scarlet Tanager, pink body/3749

Scarlet Tanager, pink body, pair/3750

Scissor-Tailed Flycatcher/3757

Shoveler Duck /3455

Summer Tanager/3868

Titmouse/3592

Turkey/3275

Vermillion Fly-Catcher/3923

Western Blue
Bird/3815

Western Tanager,
red matte body/3749

Western Tanager, red
matte body, pair/3750

White-Headed Pigeon, double/3518D

Willow Ptarmigan/3451

White Wing Crossbill/3754S

White Wing Crossbill, pair/3754D

Wilson Warbler/3597

Wren/3401S

Wren, pair/3401D

Yellow Warbler/3850

Yellow (Prothonatary)
Warbler/3447

Yellow-headed Verdin/3921

Yellow-throated
Warbler/3924

3715	Blue Jay (peanut), 10¼″	500–550
	Antique Gold	ND
	Red clay, Fulper glaze	ND
3716	Blue Jay (leaf), 10¼″	500–550
	Antique Gold	500–550
3717	Blue Jay, pair, 12½″	1000 +
3722	European Finch, 4½″	125
3746	Canary right, rose flower, 6¼″	150–200
3747	Canary left, blue flower, 6¼″	150–200
3749 S	Scarlet Tanager, pink body, 4¾″	175
3749 S	Western Tanager, red matte body, 4¾″	175–200
3750 D	Scarlet Tanager, pink body, pair, 8″	275–300
3750 D	Western Tanager, red matte body, pair, 8″	300–350
3751 S	Red-Headed Woodpecker, 6¼″	
	Pink glossy	100–125
	Red matte	125–150
	White	ND
3752 D	Red-Headed Woodpecker, pair, 7¾″	
	Pink glossy	150–175
	Red matte	175–200
3754 S	White Wing Crossbill, 3½″	
	Pink glossy	ND
	Red matte (? – none reported to date)	
3754 D	White Wing Crossbill, pair, 8¾″	
	Pink glossy	275–300
	Red matte	275–300
?	White Wing Crossbill, group (three on branch), w/yellow flowers	ND
3755 S	Audubon Warbler, 4¼″	125–150
3756 D	Audubon Warbler, pair, 7¾″	250–300
3757	Scissor-Tailed Flycatcher, 11″	450–500
3758	Magpie-Jay, 10¾″	500–550
3810	Blackpoll Warbler, 3½″	125–150
3811	Chestnut-backed Chickadee, 5″	75–100
3812	Chestnut-sided Warbler, 4″	75–100
3813	Evening Grosbeak, 5″	100–125
3814	Black-throated Green Warbler, 3⅛″	100–125
3815	Western Blue Bird, 7″	150–175
3848	Golden-crowned Kinglet, 4⅛″	75–90
3849	Goldfinch, 4″	75–100
3850	Yellow Warbler, 4″	75–100
3851	Red-breasted Nuthatch, 3¾″	60–80

3852	Cliff Swallow, 3¾″	100–125
3853	Golden-Crowned Kinglets, group, 5½″ x 5″	450–500
3868	Summer Tanager, 4″	100–125
3921	Yellow-headed Verdin, 4½″	ND
3923	Vermillion Fly-Catcher, 5¾″ tall	500
3924	Yellow-throated Warbler, 5½″	50–75
3925	Magnolia Warbler	ND

TERRA COTTA Beginning in 1974, these birds were made in a terra cotta body, not the white body usually found. I have seen one mounted on a black base and heard of other variations. They are priced the same as the hand-painted birds. This list is for information only.

Cockatoo
Indigo Bunting
Kentucky Warbler
Oriole
Parula Warbler
Titmouse
Wren
Wren, pair
Yellow Warbler

DATED BIRDS The hand-painted dated birds (1974) used a different numbering system than the earlier birds. Some collectors will not buy these, as they were made after Stangl was sold. However, they are generally priced the same as the earlier birds. This list is for information only.

90–101	Cockatoo
90–102	Kentucky Warbler
90–103	Nuthatch
90–104	Oriole
90–105	Parula Warbler
90–106	Titmouse
90–107	Wilson Warbler
90–108	Wren

MISCELLANY The planter will be found with either a green or a white gourd. The deviled-egg plate comes with either a hen or rooster (figure or shaker) attached to the center. Some collectors believe this was sold as a three-piece set,

Deviled-egg plate with hen; bird on gourd planter.

with the hen figure appropriately attached to the plate, and a set of shakers for sprinkling the eggs. Why an unusable shaker was attached is an unanswered question.

I have not been able to uncover any information about the two coasters, cut down from the standard 5″ coaster/ash tray, shown in the color section.

Bird on gourd planter	150–200
Coasters	ND
Dealer sign w/Cockatoo	ND
Deviled-egg plate	60–75

CHILDREN'S WARE

Kiddie Sets

These sets, also called Kiddieware, were made from about 1942 through the 1970s. They were available as two-piece sets (a cup and a three-compartment dish) or three-piece sets (a 9" plate, a cup and a 5½" bowl). Bowls are the hardest pieces to find, not surprising when you picture a child banging a spoon against the side of one.

All patterns were hand painted; most were hand carved. Those that never were are indicated as "nc" for "never carved" in the list below.

"Stangl kiddie sets are individually gift boxed in approved mailer cartons." "Colorful hand-out gift carton has after-use as toy suitcase." This last was only available for a while.

DECORATIONS "Favorite nursery rhyme and 'wild west' subjects." There are distinct decorations for the two-piece sets and the three-piece sets, with one exception: The Cookie Twins divided dish has the Ginger Boy on the left and the Ginger Girl on the right. The cup that goes with each set is decorated differently.

A personalized three-piece set was also available. The plate had either three ducklings on it or ABC blocks, the bowl had "All gone!"

Stangl

personalized
KIDDIE SET

in the well, and the cup had "All mine!" on the side. A child's name, in blue for a boy and pink for a girl, would be hand painted on the plate only, underneath the decoration.

A Wildlife set has turned up (see color section). Made in the mid-sixties as an exclusive for Tiffany's in New York, it was on a white body and was not carved. It had a colorful animal design that presented some production problems, specifically the frog in the bottom of the cup and the parrot perched on its handle. The bowl is an 8" coupe shape. Perhaps 250 of these sets were made.

Year of introduction when known and designers' initials are included in the listings.

ODDITIES As with other Stangl lines, curious items turn up, such as a Little Bo Peep plate with a blue verge instead of pink, and a Humpty-Dumpty plate with an olive-green, not lime green, border. A Dolphin plate and cup have been found; both are marked "Sample." Also, pieces will turn up marked for Altman's, Henri Bendel, Lunning (see different-shaped cup in color section) or Nieman-Marcus.

Pricing. A few patterns were reissued on a white body; some carved, some not, even though the pattern had originally been carved. These were made in the mid-seventies, some perhaps in the late sixties. Most had a straight-sided mug. I have listed these patterns with a /W. Pieces should be priced 10% to 20% less than prices below. Expect to pay more for a complete set.

Note: Abbreviations used in the list: KH = Kay Hackett; CC = Cleo Crawford; BP = Betty Powell; /W = White body, reissued.

ABC   Cookie Twins   Ducky Dinner

Five Little Pigs   Kitten Capers   Mealtime Special

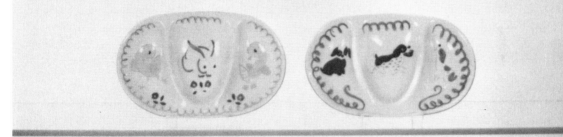

Our Barnyard Friends   Playful Pups

TWO-PIECE SETS

ABC (1956) /KH /W

Cup	30
Dish	60

Bunny Lunch (1958)

Cup	45
Dish	75

Cookie Twins (1957)

Cup	45
Dish	75

Ducky Dinner (1958) /KH

Cup	45

Dish	75

Five Little Pigs (1956)

Cup	50
Dish	80

Mealtime Special

Cup	30
Dish	60

Kitten Capers /KH

Cup	35
Dish	65

Our Barnyard Friends /KH

Cup	35

Dish	65
Playful Pups /KH	
Cup	35
Dish	65

THREE-PIECE SETS

Blue Elf (1958) /KH	
Cup	40
Bowl	55
Plate	70
Carousel/Blue border	
Cup	30
Bowl	45
Plate	60
Carousel/Pink border	
Cup	30
Bowl	45
Plate	60
Carousel/Gold border	
Cup	30
Bowl	45
Plate	60
Cat and the Fiddle (1956)	
Cup	50
Bowl	65
Plate	80
Circus Clown (1965)(nc)/W	
Cup	28
Bowl	40
Plate	55
Flying Saucer	
Cup	ND
Bowl	ND
Plate	ND
Ginger Boy (1957)	
Cup	40
Bowl	55
Plate	75
Ginger Cat (1965) /KH(nc)/W	
Cup	30
Bowl	45
Plate	60
Ginger Girl (1957)	
Cup	40
Bowl	55
Plate	70
Goldilocks /CC? #42?	
Cup	45
Bowl	60

Plate	70
Humpty-Dumpty/Blue border	
Cup	28
Bowl	40
Plate	55
Humpty-Dumpty/Pink border	
Cup	28
Bowl	40
Plate	55
Humpty-Dumpty/Lime Green border	
Cup	28
Bowl	40
Plate	55
Indian Campfire /KH	
Cup	45
Bowl	60
Grill Plate	ND
Plate	75
Jack in the Box	
Cup	28
Bowl	40
Plate	55
Little Bo Peep /KH	
Cup	25
Bowl	35
Plate	50
Little Boy Blue /W	
Cup	25
Bowl	35
Plate	50
Little Quackers (1958) /KH /W	
Cup	30
Bowl	45
Plate	60
Mary Quite Contrary (1956) /KH	
Cup	40
Bowl	55
Plate	70
Mother Goose/Blue	
Cup	45
Bowl	60
Plate	75
Mother Goose/Pink	
Cup	45
Bowl	60
Plate	75
Mother Hubbard (nc)	
Cup	28
Bowl	40

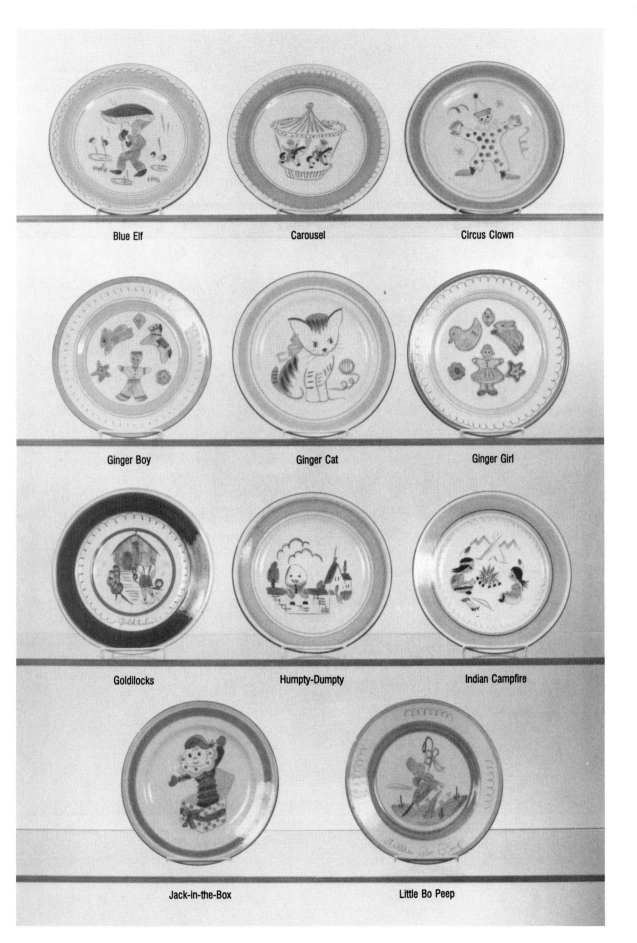

Blue Elf

Carousel

Circus Clown

Ginger Boy

Ginger Cat

Ginger Girl

Goldilocks

Humpty-Dumpty

Indian Campfire

Jack-in-the-Box

Little Bo Peep

Little Boy Blue

Little Quackers

Mary Quite Contrary

Mother Goose

Mother Hubbard

Peter Rabbit

Pink Fairy

Pony Trail

Ranger Boy

Woman in the Shoe

Plate	55
Peter Rabbit /KH	
Cup	35
Bowl	50
Plate	65
Pink Fairy (1958) /KH	
Cup	40
Bowl	55
Plate	70
Pony Trail	
Cup	35
Bowl	50
Plate	65
Ranger Boy	
Cup	35
Bowl	50
Plate	65
Wizard of Oz	
Cup	ND
Bowl	ND
Plate	ND
Woman in the Shoe (early)	
Cup	65
Bowl	50
Plate	80
Woman in the Shoe (1956)	
Cup	28
Bowl	40
Plate	55

Pet feeding dish with Ginger Cat decoration.

should be part of a set, but a cup has not yet been found. The baby's feeding dish has been found decorated with either a blue, pink or green band around the rim. The pet feeding dish has either a cat (Ginger Cat) or dog on it. Only one tile has been found; it has the Pink Carousel decoration on it. A three-part warming dish, all ceramic, with a cork-stoppered hole for adding hot water, has been found with the Little Quackers decoration.

Cup, Hans/Fritz	ND
Divided dish, Bluebirds	ND
Feeding dish, baby, 8¼″ x 1¾″ deep	ND
Feeding dish, pet	ND
Tile, round, 5½″	ND
Warming dish, Little Quackers	ND

MUSICAL MUG   During the early 1940s, Kay Hackett designed patterns for a musical mug made for Lunning: 3″ deep, on a hollow 2″-deep flared base, making it 5″ tall overall, with a large handle. Lunning added the musical device, which was placed in the base; there are three small holes or niches in the side, about ½″ from the bottom, which were used to secure the device to the mug. Only mugs without these devices have been found so far. See color section.

Jack and Jill	ND
Mary Had a Little Lamb	ND
Toy Soldiers	ND

MISCELLANY   A cup, red body, with a cartoon character (Hans or Fritz?), has been found. It is not known whether it was intended to be part of the Kiddie Ware line, or was a separate item. The divided dish with the Bluebirds

CHRISTMAS ITEMS

Christmas Cards

These ceramic "cards" were all done on the 5" coaster/ash trays. "Government work" was the term used by Stangl employees for items made expressly for Martin Stangl. Given to family, friends and business associates, approximately fifty were made in any given year.

Betty Stangl Thomas: "My dad had four wives. [He began these after] my mother had passed on and he remarried. He always did a different pattern every year and he always had, like, 'Betty and Martin Stangl, Merry Christmas,' and then it was 'Natalie and Martin Stangl.' And I said, 'Dad, since you're getting married so many times, why don't you just put Mr. and Mrs. J. M. Stangl?' He started doing that."

The cards were not dated, so we don't know how many different ones were made overall. But considering that the gold kiln was bought in 1956 (the cards all have gold on them) and Martin Stangl died in 1972, this may be a complete list.

Pricing. $60–75.

Blue bells & pine bough
Candle & pine bough
Carolers
Father Christmas (decal)
Holly (three leaves)
Holly (seven leaves)
Holly & bells
Holly & pine boughs
Jewelled Christmas tree (single)
Jewelled Christmas tree (triple)
Poinsettia
Santa (child's drawing)
Scroll
Snowman
Wreath
Wreath w/fruit

Christmas Ware

CHRISTMAS TREE (ca 1960)   This is a decal decoration. The pieces seen so far have been on the china body. Stangl also made two sizes of casseroles with this decal for another company; these will be marked "Cuthbertson USA."

Cup	12
Mug, 2 cup	25
Plate, 6"	8
Plate, 7"	10
Plate, 8"	15
Plate, 9"	20
Plate, 10"	20
w/metal handle	30
Saucer	6
Server, 2-tier	35

FATHER CHRISTMAS (ca 1960)   This is a decal decoration. The pieces seen so far have been on the china body.

Ash Tray	30
Plate, 6"	12
Plate, 7"	15
Plate, 8"	20
Plate, 10"	25
w/metal handle	30

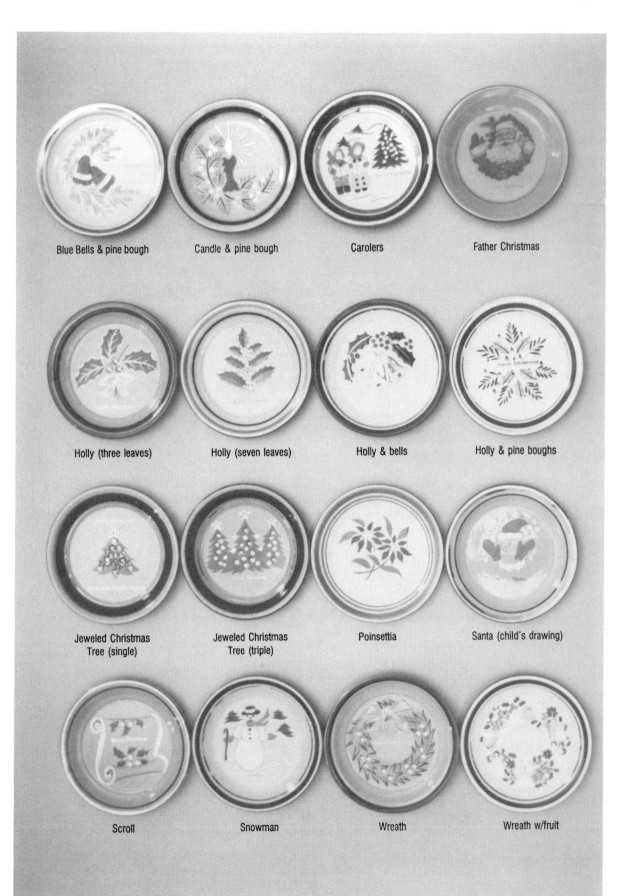

Blue Bells & pine bough

Candle & pine bough

Carolers

Father Christmas

Holly (three leaves)

Holly (seven leaves)

Holly & bells

Holly & pine boughs

Jeweled Christmas
Tree (single)

Jeweled Christmas
Tree (triple)

Poinsettia

Santa (child's drawing)

Scroll

Snowman

Wreath

Wreath w/fruit

HOLLY (1954)   Designed by Kay Hackett. Hand carved and hand painted ". . . deep green leaves accented by cherry red berries will brighten any festive setting."

Ash tray, fluted	18
Ash tray, rectangular	30
Bowl, salad, round, 10″	40
Bowl, soup, flat	25
Bowl, vegetable, round, 8″	30
Cake, footed	35
Cigarette box	40
Coaster/Ash tray	20
Creamer	18
Cup	20
Dish, cereal, 5½″	20
Dish, fruit, 5½″	15
Jug, 6 ounce	18
Jug, ½ pint	22
Jug, 1 pint	30
Jug, 1 quart	35
Jug, 2 quart	45
Mug, low	25
Mug, 2 cup	35
Plate, 6″	12
Plate, 8″	20
Plate, 10″	30
Plate, chop, 12½″	45
Saucer	10
Server, center handle	15
Sugar	20

JEWELLED CHRISTMAS WARE (TREE) (ca 1956 to late 60s/P#3957). Designed by Kay Hackett. "Created by a special Stangl process, the gold and silver tree ornaments appear to come alive on the vibrant background colors of every piece."

This pattern, with its slightly indented Christmas balls, was created for one of Martin Stangl's Christmas cards. When it was expanded into a small service, it may have been an exclusive for Carole Stupell, but later it was available nationwide. Dave Thomas explains the special process, done in green ware: "You take a small hand-held drill, a drebble, with a ball on the end of it, a little ball, smaller than a cherry, smaller than a grape, and you just touch it."

Holly plate, cup and saucer.

Kay Hackett: "We tried to work to the point where the gold could be applied maybe with a sponge tip or a Q-tip type thing and it wouldn't take. We hired a girl who had been working in gold in another pottery to come in and teach our girls how to use gold. Because it's like painting with molasses."

The person hired was Veronica Moroz, who had been working in gold at Cordey. To speed up decoration of the indented circles, they purchased ink-free felt-tip pens and ground them down to the desired size. A twist with these did the trick.

Bowl, salad, 12″	50
Cigarette box	45
Clock	50
Coaster/ash tray	20
Creamer	18
Cup	20
Cup, punch	30
Jug, 6 ounce	18
Jug, ½ pint	22
Jug, 1 pint	30
Mug, coffee, low	25
Plate, 6″	12

Left to right, top row: *Christmas Tree (decal) plate; Jewelled Christmas Tree punch cup and plate; Father Christmas plate (unusual shape).* Bottom row: *Undocumented Christmas Tree patterns, hand-painted on left, decal on right.*

Plate, 8″	20	Server, center handle	15
Plate, 10″	30	Server, two-tier	30
Saucer	10	Sugar	20

DINNERWARE

Early Dinnerware

Stangl's first dinnerware lines were made on a white body that was in production until ca 1942. The most popular of these were the #1388/Colonial and #2000/Americana shapes. Though the red body replaced the white body for dinnerware production in 1942, there is a possibility that Colonial and Americana were kept in limited production for a short while after red body production began.

In this section I have listed the known early white-bodied dinnerware. Technically, the first dinnerware line was Fulper's #901 shape, available in three of the basic Stangl dinnerware colors, and it seems a safe guess that Martin Stangl designed the shape and devised the glazes.

I have listed only those colors that have been seen; it is possible that #1080 and #1260 were discontinued before Tangerine was introduced.

Pricing. There are a number of ND prices in this section, but also items of low desirablility, as I don't believe there are many collectors who are trying to put together sets of these lines.

#1080 So far, found in Silver Green and Persian Yellow. The low shape number and the colors might indicate that this was a short-lived, early line, perhaps from the late twenties. Some pieces will be found with a combined Fulper/Stangl mark; these bring higher prices.

Bowl, salad, 12″	30
Creamer	10
Cup	8
Jug, syrup	ND
Plate, 6″	6
Plate, 10½″	10
Plate, chop, 12″	25
Saucer	4
Sugar	15
Tea pot	35

#1260 (1930) An angular, Art Deco style. So far, only seen in Silver Green, as well as some Fulper colors. Not enough pieces have been seen to price this line.

Creamer
Cup
Jug, small
Jug, large
Plate
Saucer
Sugar
Teapot

#1800 (1934) Called Leaf line, Cabbage Leaf or Lettuce. Found in early colors of ivory, maize, Silver Green, turquoise and white, and in late colors of Chartreuse, Yellow and Gloss White.

Pricing. Deduct 20% for late colors.

Bowl, salad	25
Compote, footed	20
Creamer	10
Cup	10
Plate, bread and butter	5
Plate, buffet, 20″	ND
Plate, salad	10

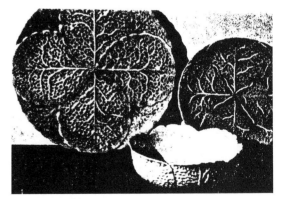

#1800 Leaf plates and bowl.

Plate, service	15
Relish, elongated	20
Relish, two part w/twig handle	15
Relish, three part	20
Saucer	3
Sugar	15

#1870/DAISY (‹1935) A flower shape, its shape number places it near the beginning of the Flower Ware line; however, only dinnerware has been seen. Made in Colonial Blue, Silver Green, Tangerine Red and Persian Yellow.

Bowl, nut, 4½″	10
Bowl, relish	20
Bowl, salad, 10½″	30
Bowl, soup, 9″	15
Bowl, soup, lug, (cream soup), 5″	15
Bowl, vegetable, oval, 10″	25
Candleholder, each	25
Compote, low, 10″	ND
Compote, high, 10″	ND
Creamer	10
Cup	12
Dish, fruit, 6″	12
Plate, 6″	8
Plate, 8″	10

Plate, 9″	15
Plate, 10″	20
Plate, chop, 14″	ND
Platter, oval, 12″	ND
Relish, 2-section, large	ND
Relish, 3-section, round	ND
Saucer	5
Sugar	15

#1902 This shape was used exclusively for Fisher, Bruce's Della Ware line, with a few exceptions. The five jugs were sold in Colonial Blue, Silver Green, Tangerine and Persian Yellow; Aqua Blue was a fifth color available on tumblers in the Beverage Set. The 9″ bowl was available in the four satin colors. See Specialty Lines/Fisher-Bruce.

Pricing. These prices are for solid colors only.

Bowl, 9″	25
Jug, ½ pint	12
Jug, 1 pint	18
Jug, 1 quart	25
Jug, w/ice lip, 2 quart	35
Tumbler	15

Left to right: *#1870 (Daisy) creamer, plate, sugar; #1260 pitcher; #1080 plate and teapot.*

#1902 tumbler and pitcher.

#1388/#2000

These were Stangl's most popular lines of dinnerware in the thirties. By 1937, #1388 was being shipped by the boxcar load to Jordan Marsh in Boston. Production was severely curtailed when the new hand-painted line was introduced in 1942, continuing for perhaps a year longer.

#1388 A fluted shape with alternating thick and thin ribs. (See also Miniatures, Treasured, Rainbow Ware and Special Items/Lunning.) Of these two lines, #1388 was brought out first, but I have not been able to pinpoint the year of introduction. It is not in Fulper's 1927 catalog, though the #901 large luncheon line is present. #1388 is well established in a 1935 listing, the next year for which I have documentation (though many pieces were still to be added in the later years of the decade). Based on the numbering system, I would guess 1930 as a likely date.

The individual casserole with stick handle is not listed in any Stangl literature. The candy dish with bird finial seems to be the small mixing bowl with a special lid. This is a guess. The tea cup is footed; the coffee cup is wider than the tea and is not footed.

Old catalogs list a number of pieces which have not been identified. They are: nut bowl, relish bowl, low footed tray, high footed tray (the latter two were listed with the compote, so they are not the same) and deep plate, the pottery industry term for a flat soup. Some of these may be alternate names for familiar items. Also, other relish and hors d'oeuvre plates may exist.

Metal Accessories. The individual bean pot, the custard and the ramekin were available in sets of six in wire trays. A 6″ bowl came with a metal frame and tongs to make an ice bowl set. A 12″ chop plate with metal handle and eight 7″ plates made up a sandwich set. A metal handle wrapped with wicker could be attached to a five-part relish dish. And a 2-quart pitcher with six mugs in a metal tray made up a beverage set.

Solid Colors/Colonial. Colonial is the name for the #1388 solid color line. Colonial Blue, Persian Yellow and Silver Green were introduced in 1924 on the original pieces of #901. The 1935 listing includes Rust, Tangerine and Surf White as well. In 1937 Aqua Blue was added and Surf White became Satin White. All of these colors were still available in 1940.

The four basic colors are Colonial Blue, Persian Yellow, Silver Green and Tangerine, which are the most easily found. Aqua Blue, Rust, Satin Brown and Satin White are harder to find, especially the last two colors. Burgundy, Satin Blue and a deep plum have been found, but there is no evidence that they were ever put into production.

Early price lists show that Tangerine was about one-third more expensive than the other colors and, in the 1940 catalog, Rust was priced at 50% above list. Sets of various sizes in all four basic colors in both Colonial and Americana lines were called Rainbow Sets.

Note: Some of the hollowware decorated in Tangerine will have a matte green interior, rather than being all-over Tangerine. If this is important to you, keep it in mind when mail ordering.

Ash tray, round, ruffled, 3¾"	ND
Ash tray/coaster, ridges in well, 3½"	12
Baking shell	15
Bean pot, one handle, 7" high	45
Bean pot, individual	18
Bottle, refrigerator, w/ pottery stopper, 9"	ND
Bowl, console, oval, 12" x 8"	25
Bowl, mixing, 5"	ND
Bowl, mixing, 7½"	ND
Bowl, mixing, 9"	ND
Bowl, mixing, 14"	ND
Bowl, salad, round, lug, 8"	20
Bowl, salad, round, lug, 10"	25
Bowl, salad, round, lug, 14"	ND
Bowl, soup, lug, 4½"	8
Bowl, soup, lug, 5"	8
w/lid	16
Bowl, vegetable, oval, 10"	15
Butter chip, 2¼"	8
Candleholder, single, 3½" tall	12
Candleholder, triple	50
Candy jar w/bird finial	ND
Carafe, w/wood handle	35
w/pottery stopper	50
Casserole, 5"	25
Casserole, 8"	35
Casserole, ind, stick handle	10
w/lid	15
Cigarette box, 4½" x 3½"	35
Coffee pot, AD, 6 cup	60
Compote, 7"	15
Creamer	10
Creamer, AD	10
Creamer, ind, 2½" high	8
Custard cup, 3½"	6
Cup	8
Cup, AD	8
Cup, coffee	9
Dish, 6"	8
Egg cup	8
Gravy faststand	20
Hors d'oeuvres, 5 part, 12"	35
Hors d'oeuvres, round, 3 part, 9"	25
Hors d'oeuvres, oval, 11½"	25
Hors d'oeuvres, oval, 18½"	ND
Jelly mold, small	ND

Left to right: *Individual casserole with stick handle; 8" oval relish; all six pitchers, including the miniature.*

Jelly mold, large	ND
Jug, 2½″ high	12
Jug, 3½″ high	12
Jug, 4½″ high	18
Jug, 5½″ high	25
Jug, 7½″ high	35
Jug, ball, ice lip	35
Jug, syrup	30
w/lid	40
Jug, waffle, 2 quart	35
w/lid	45
Mug (tumbler)	20
Pie baker, 11″	25
Plate, 6″	3
Plate, 7″	4
Plate, 8″	6
Plate, 9″	9
Plate, 10″	12
Plate, chop, 12″	20
Plate, chop, 14″	25
Plate, grill, 10″	16
Plate, grill, 11½″	20
Platter, oval, 12″	18
Platter, oval, 14″	22
Ramekin, 4″	8
Relish, 2 part, 6½″ x 7″	20
Relish, oval, 19″	ND
Saucer	3
Saucer, AD	5
Server, center handle	10
Shaker, pepper/1 hole	8
Shaker, salt/3 hole	8
Shirred egg, 8″ x 6″	15
Sugar	12
Sugar, AD	12
Sugar, ind, 2½″ high, open	8
Teapot, 6 cup	50
Teapot, individual	30
Tray/shakers	18
Tray/sugar & creamer, ind, 8″ x 4″	15
Tray/sugar & creamer, regular	15

Six-part 19″ oval relish. Early catalogs list, but do not identify, a variety of relishes and hors d'oeuvres servers.

Bean Pot with cover

Candleholder, triple

Tea set with bird finials. Note that the lids are not ribbed.

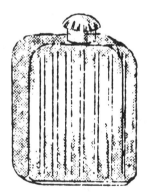

Refrigerator bottle w/stopper

Hand-painted Decorations. We do not know how many pieces of #1388 were hand painted. The list below has been compiled from every piece that has been seen, regardless of pattern. It does not necessarily follow that if a piece turns up in one pattern, it will be found in all patterns.

The number of hand-painted decorations on the #1388 shape is not known. An old flyer indicates eighteen; the ones listed below are all that are currently known, and some are just color variations of one design.

Smaller items, such as shakers, usually have color bands that match the pattern, but do not have the pattern itself.

"Argosy"/3336 Brown single-masted ship, surrounded by fish, on gold background.

Bluebell/3334 (1940) Blue flower and green leaves on yellow background w/blue rim band. The cup, sugar and creamer had the blue band only.

Crocus/KH/3343, blue flower; /3344, pink flower: both w/green leaves on white background, multicolor rim.

Five-Petal Flower/KH Three versions, all on ivory background: (1) red with green leaves; (2) yellow with green leaves; (3) blue with green leaves. Done for a firm in Boston.

"Gazelle" Brown gazelle on gray background.

Harvest/3341 A fruit design of grapes and apples.

"Lemon"/3338 Yellow lemon and green leaves outlined in blue on ivory background with green rim band.

Newport/3333 A sailboat done in shades of blue with white sails (although the teapot is white with blue sailboat). Some pieces will have only seagulls and waves.

Old Orchard/3307 Apple, grapes and leaves in blue, green and red on ivory background.

Plum Three versions: (A) green plum on green background; (B) blue plum on blue background; (C) yellow plum on tan background.

"Six-Petal Flower" Blue flower on rose background with blue rim.

"Villa" Blue, lavender and yellow house with green trees on white background.

Newport figural shakers.

	Newport	Harvest	Others
Bowl, salad, deep, 10″	45	40	35
Bowl, salad, shallow, 10″	45	40	35
Bowl, salad, 12″	50	45	40
Bowl, soup, lug, 4½″	18	15	12
Bowl, vegetable, oval, 10″	40	35	25
Candle holder	25	20	15
Carafe, w/wood handle	65	60	55
w/pottery stopper	75	70	65
Creamer	18	15	12
Cup	12	10	8
Dish, fruit, 6″	12	10	8
Plate, 6″	15	10	6
Plate, 7″	15	12	7
Plate, 8″	20	15	8
Plate, 9″	25	20	10
Plate, 10″	35	30	15
Plate, chop, 12″	50	40	30
Plate, chop, 14″	50	40	30
Saucer	8	5	3
Shaker	12	10	10
Shaker, figural, each	60	—	—
Sugar	20	18	15
Teapot	85	70	60

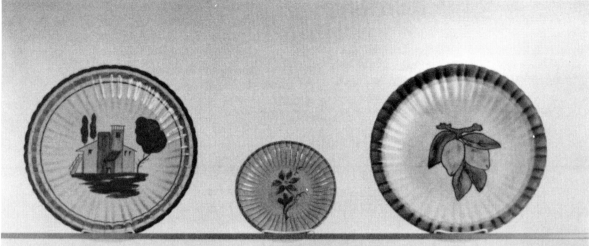

"Villa"   "Six-Petal Flower"   "Lemon"

"Argosy"   Plate w/seagulls   Teapot   Plate w/boat

Old Orchard   Harvest   Five-Petal Flower

Crocus   "Gazelle"   Bluebell

#2000 (1936) A plain round shape. Its number, 2000, will be found inscribed on the bottom. The carafe was brought out in 1938; it's hard to find, as are the ash tray and butter pat. Old price lists indicate a 12″ footed salad bowl that has not been seen; a 12″ bowl with straight sides and no foot has been seen. The Gravy Faststand is the lug soup attached to a 6″ plate. The four-footed bowl is not in Stangl's literature; it may have been made as a special-order premium.

Metal Accessories. There is a metal tray for the shakers, and a tray that holds four ash trays. A 2-quart pitcher and six mugs in a wire carrier made up a beverage set.

Solid Colors/Americana. The #2000 solid color line is called Americana. "Particularly suited for Colonial and Modern furniture." Made in four solid colors: Colonial Blue, Silver Green, Tangerine and Persian Yellow.

Ash tray, 4″	12
Bowl, lug, 4″	7
Bowl, salad, 7″	12
Bowl, salad, 10″	30
Bowl, salad, 11½″	35
Bowl, soup, coupe, 7½″	10
Bowl, soup, lug, 5″	8
w/lid	18
Bowl, vegetable, oval, 8″	20
Bowl, vegetable, oval, 10″	20
Butter pat	ND
Carafe w/wooden handle	35
w/pottery stopper	50
Coffee pot, AD	50
Creamer	6
Creamer, individual	10
Cup	8
Cup, AD	9
Cup, coffee	9
Cup, cream soup, 2 open handles, 5″	10
Dish, fruit, 5½″	7

Clockwise from top center: *Jug, mug (tumbler), ash tray, butter pat, unlisted bowl with inturned rim, 4″ lug bowl, fruit dish, 5½″ lug soup, shakers, sugar, creamer and teapot.*

Gravy Faststand	15
Jug, ball w/ice lip	35
Jug, ½ pint	15
Jug, 1 pint	20
Jug, 1 quart	25
Jug, 2 quart, ice lip w/handle wrapped	35
w/lid	50
Mug (tumbler)	12
Plate, 6″	3
Plate, 7″	4
Plate, 8″	6
Plate, 9″	7
Plate, 10″	9
Plate, chop, 12″	25
Plate, chop, 14″	35
Platter, oval, 12″	10
Platter, oval, 14″	15
Relish, 2-section	6
Saucer	2
Saucer, AD	4
Saucer, coffee	3
Saucer, cream soup	4
Shakers, pair	16
w/metal holder	36
Sugar	10
w/bird finial	20
Sugar, open, individual	10
Teapot, 6 cup	35
Teapot, 8 cup	40
Tray, sugar/creamer, 4¼″ x 8¼″	8

Hand-Painted Decorations. As there were no candleholders in the #2000 shape, Spiral candleholders were used with some of these patterns. They, the butter pats, the shakers—and perhaps other small items—will be found only with colored bands that match the patterns.

As with #1388, the number of hand-painted decorations on #2000 is unknown. The following are all the known patterns. A question mark indicates the number is unknown.

Apple/3201 Blue apple with brown highlight on blue ground with brown band.

Cherry/3202 Blue and brown cherries on blue background.

Cosmos/3339 Pink and blue flowers with green leaves on ivory; yellow and blue bands.

"Daisies" /3346, blue flowers; /3347, pink flowers; /?, brown flowers: all with green leaves on ivory background.

Field Daisy /3306, blue flower; /?, yellow flower (this color made exclusively for Carole Stupell).

"Floral Plaid"/3316 Brown branch with green and yellow on ivory with blue plaid.

"Flower Pot"/3332 Brown flower pot with brown star-shaped flowers and blue leaves on blue with dark blue band.

Figural Ranger shakers.

Figural Daisy shakers with both yellow and blue centers.

"Laurel"/3337 Blue laurel leaves on ivory with brown and blue band.

"Plum"/3203 Three blue and white plums on yellow with pink rim.

"Poplar Flower"/3319 Pale poplar flower with brown highlights and brown leaf and a medium green rim.

Ranger/3304 (Also called Cowboy and Cactus.) A cowboy design in shades of blue, brown and marigold yellow. Some pieces have the cactus only. Attributed to Tony Sarg.

"Tropic Isle"/3320 Green and brown palm tree with sun on yellow background.

Stamped fruit decorations with hand-painted trim will also be found.

Pricing. I have priced only those pieces of Ranger known to exist. Please let me know if you find others.

	Ranger	Others
Bowl, oval, 10″	65	25
Bowl, salad, 7″	–	15
Bowl, salad, 10″	–	35
Bowl, salad, 11½″	–	40
Bowl, soup, coupe	–	12
Butter pat	–	ND
Candleholder, each	25	18
Carafe, w/wood handle	125	40
w/pottery stopper	150	50
Creamer	40	12
Cup	35	8
Cup, coffee	35	12
Cup, AD	–	18
Dish, fruit	25	12
Dish, lug, 5″	25	12
Plate, 6″	20	6
Plate, 7″	–	7
Plate, 8″	50	8
Plate, 9″	65	10
Plate, 10″	75	25
Plate, chop, 12″	125	45
Platter, oval, 12″	65	25
Saucer	15	3
Saucer, AD	–	4
Shaker, each	–	10
Shaker, figural, Field Daisy, each	–	25
Shaker, figural, Ranger, each	75	–
Sugar	50	15
Teapot	125	60

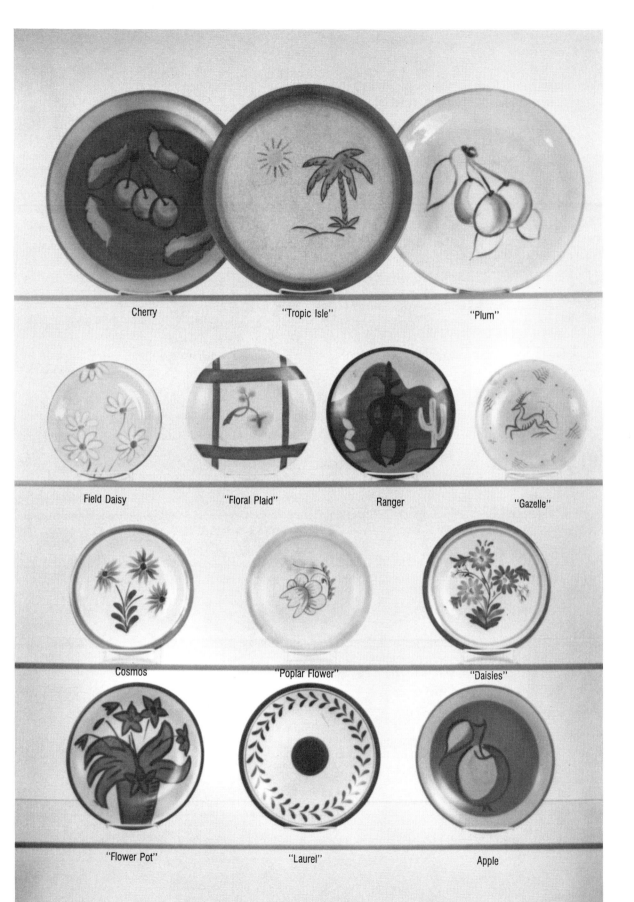

Cherry

"Tropic Isle"

"Plum"

Field Daisy

"Floral Plaid"

Ranger

"Gazelle"

Cosmos

"Poplar Flower"

"Daisies"

"Flower Pot"

"Laurel"

Apple

Hand-Painted Dinnerware

In 1942, Stangl introduced a new line of dinnerware with new shapes and decorations.

Dave Thomas: "Mr. Stangl had a theory, he's told me this many times, I can almost quote it verbatim. What you want to do is make what the other guy doesn't make, can't make or doesn't want to make, but which has salability: if it's attractive it will sell. For example, other potteries made a hand-painted dinnerware; they hand-painted on white. And he says, 'That's blah.'

"So he picked up the Pennsylvania Dutch red body, native body [Stangl had been using this on Terra Rose]. Use of an engobe goes back hundreds of years. The purpose of engobe, of course, is to change the color of the stage on which you decorate. Sgraffitto, which is the term for carving, is an old Italian art concept. He combined the red body of the Pennsylvania Dutch, the sgraffitto and the underglaze."

PROCESS First the piece is formed and allowed to dry. At this stage it is brittle and must be handled carefully. Next the engobe is applied by hand. "Engobe is a white clay body used to cover the base red body for the purpose of providing a distinctive background" for decorating. Dave Thomas: "We started off, the engobe was handpainted [brushed on]. You've seen them with their splotches of white. We got through talking with Hawley [the sales manager], we found out there were many, many customer complaints. People who didn't appreciate the fact that there's a fading in the engobe so the body would show through . . . so we went to spraying the engobe around 1952, '53." Spraying created an even surface.

Within a day (while the engobe was still moist; it would crack if it were too dry), the piece was carved. First, the carver would place a stencilled mask over the piece and dust it. Dave Thomas: "The dust is charcoal, which has been put in a dry ball mill and ground up to a powder.

Carver's sample.

And it's put in a cloth sack [a silk stocking was used] and dusted. The carvers would be covered with that black powder, by the end of the day they looked like hell." This would leave an outline for them to follow. A carver's sample was also available for comparison.

Next, the carving was done, deep enough so that the red body showed through the engobe. Dave Thomas: "We gave the carvers a stylus, which consisted of a very thin round piece of metal, and put it on a grindstone and sharpened it. If the carvers use it for a period of time, of course, it wears down and pretty soon the lines start being from that [thin] to much wider, which changes the effect of it altogether.

"And we worked on it. I looked into carbide steel, all sorts of things and couldn't come up with it. One day one of the carvers came in and said she had a suggestion. She took an ordinary automatic pencil and put a phonograph needle in. [KH: The points were rounded off by rubbing against the concrete floor.] That answered it. If it [wears down], she'd throw the needle away and buy a needle, a thousand for a dime."

Next, the piece received its first firing, and then was sent to the decorating department. Dave Thomas: "The decorators were girls brought in off the street. They were given an aptitude test, and if they had any ability, after a week or two, they would go on piece work and they were on their own."

The painting was done freehand within the carved outlines. Immediately after, a transparent glaze was sprayed on, then the piece was fired a second time, hardening the glaze and creating a glasslike surface.

AVAILABILITY Patterns were seldom discontinued. Per a flyer picturing 28 patterns: "All patterns illustrated here are inactive, that is, they are not produced daily. When ordering inactive patterns, place on separate orders and allow 6–8 weeks for delivery." Orders were accumulated and these inactive patterns were manufactured four times a year.

Pricing. It is condition that determines price. Many pieces marked as seconds were actually firsts. Dave Thomas: "That's right. Let's take

the 14″ chop plate at fifteen dollars. That was the advertised price that Macy's would charge. Macy's got a fifty percent discount on that. Now that same plate, if it would go to Flemington, he [Stangl] would sell it for nine to ten dollars which was less than the recognized department stores.

"So many's the time we at the factory would get a call from Flemington, 'Send up some Garden Flower cups. We need about two hundred.' 'Well, we don't have any.' Merril Bacheler [Flemington Manager] would call Mr. Stangl, say, 'We can't get any from the factory.' So Stangl would go down and he'd see orders going to Marshall Field, Macy's, the big ones, take the cups right the hell out of first orders, put them in a box, and send them up there because selling them as firsts, he'd get two-fifty, selling them up to Flemington, he gets three bucks."

SHAPES When this dinnerware was introduced in 1942, Stangl used a rim shape (#3434), but added a coupe shape around 1948. The rim shape was revised (#5129) around 1962. Irene Sarnecki: "Yeah, smaller rim, they thought it was more contemporary and it gave a wider area for food, the other sort of limited you 'cause it had such a wide rim." The basic items in these shapes are illustrated in photos that follow. In addition, there were a number of generic pieces used with both the rim and coupe shape. What follows are some notes to help you understand what you find.

Ash Trays/Cigarette Boxes The Cigarette Box (3¾″ x 4½″) and the Coaster/Ash Tray (5″) are standard. In some patterns, a rectangular ash tray (3½″ x 8½″) with cigarette rests down the center or a fluted ash tray (5″) will be found.

Bowls The oval divided vegetable will be found with either rounded or slightly squared-off ends.

Casseroles There are three styles of casserole, one open, two covered. The open casserole has a stick handle and is referred to as "skillet" or "frypan" by collectors. It was made in 6″ and 8″ diameters. Of the two covered styles, one is flat-topped and has lug handles

43

on the lid and base; it was made in 6″ and 8″ diameters (a 4″ version will be found in Morning Blue and Yellow Flower). Another is dome lidded, with a knob finial, and was made in 4″ and 8″ diameters. The 4″ was used as an individual casserole and the 8″ was called a covered vegetable. Finally, another individual casserole has a lid, a stick handle and is 6″ in diameter.

Coffee pots   Stangl made 8-cup, 4-cup and individual coffee pots. In most of the patterns, the individual coffee is the same shape as the larger ones, but in some it looks like a tea pot. To avoid confusion, I have listed these as individual teapots. The coffee server is the Casual shape.

Dishes   The cereal and fruit dishes are both 5½″ in diameter but the fruit is shallower than the cereal.

Mugs   These came in several styles. The low is 9 ounces. The 2-cup came with straight sides or slightly tapered sides. A stack mug was introduced in the late sixties and sold in Flemington. It will be found with a variety of decorations, including some late dinnerware patterns.

Pitchers   These first appear in Fulper catalogs of the twenties and were used with both rim and coupe shapes until the rim shape was revised.

Plates   Of the plates, 9″ can be the hardest to find. The 7″ plate was not made in all patterns. Many 7″ plates will be white bodied because they were added ca 1965. A #1388 11½″ grill plate was used for a few patterns; Stangl called it a steak plate. Clocks have been made by Stangl, as well as by others who just used Stangl plates. When a clock is listed, it is one specifically made by Stangl.

Servers   Servers (center handle, 2-tier, 3-tier) as well as cake stands and compotes (pedestals were epoxied on) were made in Flemington and Trenton, and sold at the outlet to get additional sales mileage from standard pieces such as plates, soup bowls and vegetable bowls. Center-handle servers were also sold nationally.

Shakers   Apple Delight had apple-shaped shakers. The cylindrical shaker was used in some of the forties patterns, then dropped and brought back in the sixties. The pepper mill (an individual sugar with wooden base and top) has been reported in a few patterns but confirmed only in Country Life and Wild Rose.

Sherbet   This is called a wine goblet by some collectors.

Tiles   Tiles were made in three shapes—octagonal, round and square—in either red or white body (all 6″). Some tiles were made by Wenczel Tiles for Stangl, but I have listed only those made by Stangl.

Trays   There are four trays/dishes. The 13″ condiment, with indentations for the two cruets and two shakers, the 10½″ pickle and the 14½″ bread are the same shape. The 11″ relish is wider at one end.

MASTER LIST   Following is a master list of Stangl's hand-painted dinnerware patterns for quick reference. It gives you, when known, the date of introduction, the pattern number (P#), and the designer's initials (CC = Cleo Crawford, KH = Kay Hackett, MS = Martin Stangl, BP = Betty Powell, IS = Irene Sarnecki). Some of the dates come from company records which can be contradictory.

This list will also tell you if there is an individual price list for the pattern (following this list alphabetically; every known piece is listed), or whether the pattern is included in the group pricing, which follows the alphabetical listings. And I have included descriptions for obscure patterns.

Hand-painted patterns on #1388 (except Treasured below) and #2000 shapes are in Dinnerware/Early. If a pattern name doesn't appear in that section or here, please check the index.

Three patterns made up a line called Casual: Maple Whirl, Rustic and Spun Gold. "Stangl's charming casual dinnerware . . . designed to meet the increasing desire for casual, informal dining. The consumer-selected colors will blend with most any decor." Company folders show the same sixteen pieces available in each of the three decorations.

After the 1965 fire, the glaze used on Blue Daisy could not be made, so a clear glaze was used, the scroll border dropped, and the name changed to Bachelor Button. The Golden Harvest (yellow flower) and the Pink Lily (pink flower) decoration is the same except for the flower color. Piecrust and Sunshine are the same design in different colors.

A device I use to distinguish the spelling (which might be confusing) between Windfall the dinner set and Wind Fall the salad set is: Windfall the dinner set has the small "f" and the small leaves, Wind Fall the salad set has the large "F" and the large leaves. And be careful not to confuse the 1942 Tulip/Yellow with Yellow Tulip, a late pattern.

Adrian /IS. See Stoneware.

Amber Glo (1954/P#3899) /KH. Ind list.

Antigua (1971) /IS. See Stoneware.

Apple Delight (1965/P#5161) /KH. Carved border only. Group list 1.

Aztec (P#5222) /IS. Black, white and turquoise, made for someone in New York. Group list 2.

Bachelor Button (1965) /IS. Group list 1.

Bamboo (1974). Design on flatware, solid color hollowware. Group list 2.

Bella Rosa (1960) /KH. Group list 1.

Bittersweet (1962/P#5111) /IS. Group list 1.

Blossom Ring (1969/P#5215) /IS. See Prestige.

Blueberry (1950/P#3770) /KH. Ind list.

Blue Daisy (1963/4/P#5131) /IS. Group list 1.

Blue Melon (1974). Pattern of facing half-moons in blue and green. Group list 2.

Carnival (1954/P#3900) /KH. Use Amber Glo price list.

Chicory (1960) /KH. Ind list.

Colonial Dogwood (1968). See Prestige.

Colonial Rose (1970). Ind list.

Colonial Silver (P#5218). A short line of dinnerware was made in this decoration, in addition to the giftware. Group list 2.

Concord (1957) /KH (P#3964). See Prestige.

Country Garden (1956) /KH (P#3943). Ind list.

Country Life (1956/P#3946). Ind list.

Cranberry /KH. Group list 1.

Dahlia (P#5220). See Prestige.

Delmar (1971) /IS. See Stoneware.

Diana (1972) /IS. See Stoneware.

Fairlawn, originally named Caprice: (1959/P#4068) /KH Group list 1.

Festival (1961/P#5072). Same as Della Ware pattern. Group list 1.

First Love (1968) /IS. Group list 1.

Flora (1947/P#3768) /MS. Group list 1.

Florentine, originally named Heritage: (1958/P#4031) /KH. See Prestige.

Florette (1961/P#5073) /BP. Group list 2.

Frosted Fruit (1957/P#3963) /KH. See Prestige.

Fruit (1942/P#3697) /KH. Ind list.

Fruit and Flowers (1958/P#4030) /KH. Ind list.

Galaxy (‹1970/P#5225) /IS. Olive-green variation of Mediterranean. Group list 2.

Garden Flower (1942/P#3700) /KH. Ind list.

Garland (1959/P#4067) /KH. Ind list.

Golden Blossom (1964/P#5155) /IS. Carved border only. Group list 1.

Golden Grape (1963/P#5129) /IS. Group list 1.

Golden Harvest (1953/P#3887) /KH. Use Magnolia price list.

Grape (ca 1973). Group list 1.

Holly. See Christmas Ware

Inspiration (1968) /IS. See Prestige.

Jonquil. Group list 1.

Lyric (1954/P#3896) /KH. Ind list.

Magnolia (1952/P#3870) /KH. Ind list.

Maple Whirl (1965) /KH. "Rich, vibrant maple tones with a contrasting, woodsy green border." Group list 2.

Mediterranean (1965/P#5186). Group list 1.

Monterey (‹1970/P#5224) /IS. Rust-brown variation of Mediterranean. Group list 2.

Morning Blue (1971) /IS. Stangl advertised this as Red Stoneware; it had a reddish-brown slip sprayed over the body, decorated with a blue flower with yellow center. Rim shape. See also Yellow Flower. Group list 2.

Mountain Laurel (1947/P#3745) /CC. Ind list.

Orchard Song (1962/P#5110) /IS. Not carved. Group list 1.

Paisley (1962/P#5130) /IS. Group list 2.

Petite Flowers (1970) /IS. See Colonial Rose price list.

Piecrust (1969) /IS. Blue and turquoise flower. This shape will also be found decorated in all three Terra Rose colors. See Sunshine below. Ind list.

Pink Cosmos (1966). See Prestige.

Pink Dogwood /KH. See Prestige.

Pink Lily (1953) /KH. Group list 2.

Posies (1974). Group list 2.

Prelude (1948/P#3769). Group list 1.

Provincial (1957/P#3966) /KH. Group list 1.

Red Ivy (P#3961) /KH. See Prestige.

Ringles (1974). Group list 2.

Rooster (1970/P#5223) /IS. Ind list.

Roxanne (1972) /IS. See Stoneware.

Rustic (1965) /KH. "Chocolate browns touched with tawny caramel accents." Group list 2.

Rustic Garden (1972) See Stoneware.

Scandinavia Red body, no engobe. Black lightly sponged around edges. Clear gloss glaze. Also used on giftware. Group list 2.

Sculptured Fruit (1966/P#5179). See Prestige.

Sesame /IS. See Stoneware.

Sgraffito (1973). This is the Fruit and Flowers pattern. The red body is sprayed with a white engobe, carved and then covered with a clear glaze. It is not hand-painted. Group list 1.

Sierra (P#5221). See Prestige.

Spun Gold (1965) /KH. "Spinning swirls of sunny gold accented by a rich, green border." Group list 2.

Stardust (1968). Group list 1.

Star Flower (1952/P#3864) /KH. Ind list.

Sun Pebbles. See Stoneware.

Sunshine (P#5217) /IS. Yellow and orange flower on Piecrust shape. See Piecrust price list.

Susan (1972). See Stoneware.

Terra Rose Coupe shape dinnerware and other items will be found. Group list 2.

Thistle (1951/P#3847) /KH. Ind list.

Tiger Lily (1957/P#3965) /KH. Group list 1.

Town and Country (1974) /IS. Ind list.

Treasured. Antique Gold on the #1388 shape. Group list 2.

Trinidad (1971). See Stoneware.

Tulip/Blue (1942/P#3637) /KH. Ind list.

Tulip/Yellow (1942/P#3637) /KH. Ind list.

Water Lily (1949) /KH. Group list 1.

White Dogwood (1964/P#5167) /IS. See Prestige.

White Grape (1966). White embossed grapes and leaves on a blue background. Only eight dinnerware items, plus candy, cigarette and jewel boxes, were made. Group list 2.

Wild Rose (1955/P#3929) /KH. Ind list.

Wildwood (1957). See Prestige.

Willow (1949) /KH. Group list 2.

Windfall (1955/P#3930) /KH. Group list 1.

Wood Rose. See Stoneware.

Yankee Doodle (1974). No information available. Group list 2.

Yellow Flower 1971) /IS. Red stoneware, same shape and assortment as Morning Blue, but with a different flower, yellow plus other smaller flowers on the red/brown background. Group list 2.

Yellow Tulip. This started off in the stoneware line and then was put on the coupe shape. Group list 1.

White Grape; although this is not a hand-painted pattern, I've included it here for identification.

AMBER GLO Designed by Kay Hackett: "I was influenced by modern Scandinavian design . . . this was originally done as blue flame and instead of being grays and oranges, there were blues, like a gas flame, and yellow-orange like candles.

"We worked with *House and Garden* and they would give us a bunch of color chips, and if we used their colors for that year, they would give us this free advertising. They would make an article about Stangl, we wouldn't have to pay for it. We would have an ad in the back and we would pay for it. So, they said, use gray. That's why this pattern had gray in it. And that sold pretty well, and it was mix and match with Golden Harvest."

Amber Glo standard jug and Casual platter.

Bowl, salad, 10″	30
Bowl, salad, 12″	35
Bowl, soup, coupe, 7½″	10
Bowl, soup, lug, 5½″	9
Bowl, vegetable, covered, 8″	35
Bowl, vegetable, divided	30
Bowl, vegetable, round, 8″	20
Butter dish	30
Casserole, 6″	20
Casserole, 8″	40
Casserole, individual, knob, 4″	15
Casserole, individual, stick, 6″	15
Casserole w/handle, 6″	20
Casserole w/handle, 8″	25
Cigarette box, 3¾″ x 4½″	30
Coaster/Ash tray	8
Coffee pot, individual	45
Coffee pot, 4 cup	40
Coffee pot, 8 cup	40
Coffee server	45–50
Coffee warmer	18
Creamer	8
Creamer, Casual	15
Creamer, individual	12
Cruet	25
Cup	7
Dish, cereal, 5½″	9

Dish, fruit, 5½″	9
Dish, pickle	15
Dish, relish	18
Egg cup	8
Gravy boat	15
Gravy boat stand	8
Mug, coffee, low	15
Pitcher, 6 ounce	15
Pitcher, ½ pint	18
Pitcher, 1 pint	20
Pitcher, 1 quart	25
Pitcher, 2 quart	35
Plate, 6″	4
Plate, 8″	9
Plate, 9″	9
Plate, 10″	10
Plate, 11″	15
Plate, chop, 12½″	20
Plate, chop, 14½″	25
Platter, Casual, 13¾″	35
Saucer	2
Server, center handle	6
Shaker	8
Sugar	12
Sugar, Casual	15
Sugar, individual	12
Teapot	35
Tray, bread	25
Tray, condiment	20

BLUEBERRY Designed by Kay Hackett. "Plump, hand-carved, hand-painted blueberries that look good enough to eat." Kay Hackett: "I did the 10″ plate and somebody else adapted. I sent the design in [as a freelancer]. Where I had it going one way, they did it another. There is no way I would have done the coffee pot that way. It bothered me. But that's a difference in thinking." The mixing bowls are carved.

Pricing. Seconds were decorated in shades of blue only; 25–50% less for these items.

Blueberry demonstration plate, warmer and plate.

Ash tray, rectangular	30
Bowl, mixing, 4″	12
Bowl, mixing, 5½″	20
Bowl, mixing, 7″	25
Bowl, mixing, 9″	35
Bowl, salad, 10″	38
Bowl, salad, 12″	50
Bowl, soup, coupe, 7½″	20
Bowl, soup, lug, 5½″	15
Bowl, vegetable, covered, 8″	60
Bowl, vegetable, divided, oval/rect	40
Bowl, vegetable, round, 8″	35
Butter dish	35
Casserole, 6″	28
Casserole, 8″	60
Casserole, individual, knob, 4″	14
Casserole w/handle, 6″	22
Casserole w/handle, 8″	30
Chip 'n' Dip (nc)	50
Coaster/Ash tray	10
Coffee, individual	50
Coffee pot, 4 cup	45
Coffee pot, 8 cup	60
Coffee server	65
Coffee warmer	20
Creamer	15
Creamer, individual	15
Cruet	35
Cup	10
Cup, jumbo	40
Dish, cereal, 5½″	18
Dish, fruit, 5½″	15
Dish, pickle	18

Dish, relish	25
Egg cup	10
Gravy boat	20
Gravy boat stand	12
Mug, coffee, 2 cup	25
Pitcher, 6 ounce	15
Pitcher, ½ pint	20
Pitcher, 1 pint	25
Pitcher, 1 quart	35
Pitcher, 2 quart	50
Plate, 6″	7
Plate, 8″	12
Plate, 9″	12
Plate, 10″	18
Plate, 11″	25
Plate, chop, 12½″	35
Plate, chop, 14½″	40
Platter, Casual, 13¾″	35
Platter, oval, 14¾″	35
Saucer	6
Saucer, jumbo	10
Server, center handle	12
Shaker	10
Sugar	15
Sugar, individual	15
Teapot	50
Tray, bread	35
Tray, condiment	20

CHICORY Designed by Kay Hackett. "On the way out [to Ohio], between Batavia and Buffalo, the sides of the road were just blue with chicory, and I don't think I'd ever seen so much chicory before. It just hung in my mind and eventually I made a pattern of it."

Bowl, salad, 10″	35
Bowl, salad, 12″	50
Bowl, soup, coupe, 7½″	15
Bowl, soup, lug, 5½″	12
Bowl, vegetable, divided	35
Bowl, vegetable, round, 8″	30
Butter dish	35
Casserole, 6″	28
Casserole, 8″	55
Casserole, individual, knob, 4″	16
Casserole w/handle, 6″	20
Casserole w/handle, 8″	30
Coaster/Ash tray	10
Coffee pot, 8 cup	50
Coffee warmer	20
Creamer, old style	10
Creamer, revised	10
Cruet	30
Cup	10
Dish, cereal, 5½″	15
Dish, fruit, 5½″	12
Dish, pickle	20
Dish, relish	25
Egg cup	10
Gravy boat	20
Gravy boat stand	10
Mug, coffee, 2 cup	25
Pitcher, 6 ounce	10
Pitcher, ½ pint	20
Pitcher, 1 pint	25
Pitcher, 1 quart	30
Pitcher, 2 quart	40
Plate, 6″	6
Plate, 8″	12
Plate, 9″	12
Plate, 10″	15
Plate, 11″	20
Plate, chop, 12½″	30
Plate, chop, 14½″	40
Platter, Casual, 13¾″	45
Saucer	5
Server, center handle	10
Shaker	10
Sugar, old style	15
Sugar, revised	15
Teapot	45
Tray, bread	35

Chicory plate and divided vegetable.

COLONIAL ROSE/PETITE FLOWERS Shape designed by Rudy Kleinbeckel. Some of the pieces in Petite Flower have a turquoise band only, no flower. These are indicated with /P (for Plain) in my listing.

Bowl, salad, round, 10″	35
Bowl, salad, round, 10″ /P	25
Bowl, soup, coupe, 7½″	12
Bowl, soup, coupe, 7½″ /P	8
Bowl, soup, lug, 5½″	12
Bowl, soup, lug, 5½″ /P	8
Bowl, vegetable, round, 8″	25
Bowl, vegetable, round, 8″ /P	15
Cake stand	20
Creamer	10
Cup	10
Dish, cereal	12
Dish, cereal /P	8
Dish, fruit	12
Dish, fruit /P	8
Pitcher, ½ pint	20
Pitcher, 1 pint	25
Pitcher, 1 quart	30
Pitcher, 2 quart	35
Mug, 2 cup	25
Plate, 6″	6
Plate, 8″	10
Plate, 10″	15
Plate, chop, 12½″	30
Saucer	4
Server, center handle	10
Server, 2-tier	25
Server, 3-tier	30
Shaker	10
Sugar	15
Teapot	45
Tray for shakers	10
Tray, oval, soup indent, 8″	10
Tray, oval, soup indent, 8″ /P	5

Colonial Rose cup and mug; Petite Flowers plate.

COUNTRY GARDEN Designed by Kay Hackett. "Yellow jonquils, bluebells, buttercups make every place setting a delight." "And different flowers on every piece make each place setting a perennial nosegay!"

Country Garden teapot, 6" individual casserole with stick handle, creamer, sugar and plate.

Ash tray, fluted, 5" (nc)	10
Bowl, salad, 10"	40
Bowl, salad, 12"	55
Bowl, soup, coupe, 7½"	20
Bowl, soup, lug, 5½"	15
Bowl, vegetable, divided	35
Bowl, vegetable, round, 8"	30
Butter dish	35
Cake stand	30
Casserole, 8"	50
Casserole, individual, stick	25
Casserole w/handle, 6"	25
Casserole w/handle, 8"	35
Cigarette Box, 3¾" x 4½"	40
Clock, plain	35
Clock, ruffled	45
Coaster/Ash tray	12
Coaster/Ash tray (nc)	10
Coffee pot, 4 cup	50
Coffee pot, 8 cup	55
Coffee pot, filter	75
Coffee warmer	20
Creamer	10
Creamer, individual	12
Cruet	30
Cup	10
Dish, cereal, 5½"	15
Dish, fruit, 5½"	13
Dish, pickle	20
Dish, relish	25
Egg cup	12
Gravy boat	20
Gravy boat stand	12
Mug, coffee, low	15
Mug, coffee, 2 cup	30
Pitcher, 6 ounce	15
Pitcher, ½ pint	20
Pitcher, 1 pint	25

Pitcher, 1 quart	30
Pitcher, 2 quart	45
Plate, 6"	6
Plate, 7"	8
Plate, 8"	12
Plate, 9"	12
Plate, 10"	18
Plate, 11"	35
Plate, chop, 12½"	35
Plate, chop, 14½"	45
Plate, grill (nc)	20
Plate, party, 8" (nc)	6
Plate, party, 10" (nc)	8
Platter, Casual, 13¾"	40
Platter, oval, 14¾"	40
Sauce boat	20
Saucer	5
Saucer for mug	10
Server, center handle	10
Server, 2-tier	25
Server, 3-tier	35
Shaker	10
Sugar	16
Sugar, individual	12
Teapot	50
Tray, bread	40
Tray, condiment	22

COUNTRY LIFE Designed by Kurt Weise, adapted by Kay Hackett. Kay Hackett: "I worked on it but the originals were all done by Kurt Weise, a friend of Mr. Stangl. I warmed the whole thing up. What he had was mostly blues and French green and brown. And it was just too quiet. And I put the yellows into it and the oranges, and sharpened the greens up and changed the border and put yellow and brown in a different way and spread it over more pieces than had been made when he was there."

Generally, each piece has a different decoration on it, though some are repeated (egg cup and shaker have the same duckling; creamer and cup have the same hen; and the salad and coupe soup have the same duck).

Some pieces have alternate decorations, as listed. It is thought that the original decorations on these items were not cost effective and they were simplified. For example, the 1956 price list pictures the soup with the two ducks, the harder-to-find decoration. The one duck takes less labor to produce. A variant 12½" chop has a vegetable garden in the lower left quadrant.

The 14½" chop could be customized with the name of an individual farm.

Coaster /Duckling	20
Bowl, salad, round, 10"/Pig at fence	100
Bowl, vegetable, divided/Duck and ducklings	100
Bowl, vegetable, round, 8"/Mallard w/green head	60
Bowl, vegetable, round, 8"/Calf, chained, rearing hind legs	85
Creamer/Hen	40
Cup/Hen	35
Dish, fruit, 5½"/Pony	35
Dish, fruit, 5½"/Rooster	25
Egg cup/Chick	35
Plate, 6"/Rooster	15
Plate, 8"/Pig at fence	45
Plate, 8"/Cow standing in grass	60
Plate, 10"/Farmer's wife harvesting carrots	50
Plate, 10"/Rooster	25
Plate, 11"/Farmer baling hay	50
Plate, chop, 12½"/Farmhouse	100
Plate, chop, 14½"/Barn	125
w/farm name	150
Platter, Casual/Hen and ducklings	75
Saucer/Three little eggs	10
Shaker/Duckling	35
Soup, coupe, 8"/Mallard w/green head, centered	40
Soup, coupe, 8"/Mallard w/green head, on right, facing duck's rear sticking out of the water	75
Sugar/Rooster	50
Tray, bread/Hen with chicks	100

Left to right: *Country Life pepper mill, sugar, creamer and egg cups. Note that chicks on egg cups face either left or right. Question: The mills use the individual sugar bottoms; why have no individual sugars been found?*

FRUIT Designed by Kay Hackett. Various combinations of apple, cherry, grape, peach, pear and plum. "A natural freshness imparted by lovely fruits for dining pleasure." This began as a salad set, and was expanded to a full dinnerware line around 1945. There are two styles of cups.

Ash tray, fluted, 5″ (nc)	10
Bean pot, 2 handle (nc)	60
Bowl, mixing, 4″ (nc)	12
Bowl, mixing, 5½″ (nc)	20
Bowl, mixing, 7″ (nc)	25
Bowl, mixing, 9″ (nc)	35
Bowl, salad, 10″	40
Bowl, salad, 11″	45
Bowl, salad, 12″ (nc)	50
Bowl, soup, coupe, 7½″	20
Bowl, soup, lug, 5½″	15
Bowl, vegetable, covered, 8″	65–70
Bowl, vegetable, divided, oval, 8″	40
Bowl, vegetable, divided, round, 10″	40
Bowl, vegetable, round, 8″	32
Butter dish	40
Cake stand	25
Casserole, 6″	25
Casserole, 8″	55
Casserole, individual, stick	25
Casserole w/handle, 6″	25
Casserole w/handle, 8″	35
Cigarette Box	65–75
Clock	45
Coaster/Ash tray (nc)	10
Coffee pot, 4 cup	60
Coffee pot, 8 cup	60
Coffee warmer	20
Creamer	10
Creamer, individual	12
Cruet	30
Cup (leaf decoration)	10
Cup (peach decoration)	12
Cup, Jumbo	40
Dish, cereal, 5½″	15
Dish, fruit, 5½″	12
Dish, pickle	20
Dish, relish	25
Egg cup	10
Gravy boat	22
Gravy boat stand	15
Mug, coffee, low	15

Mug, coffee, 2 cup	30
Pitcher, 6 ounce	15
Pitcher, ½ pint	20
Pitcher, 1 pint	25
Pitcher, 1 quart	35
Pitcher, 2 quart	45
Plate, 6″	6
Plate, 7″	10
Plate, 8″	13
Plate, 9″	15
Plate, 10″	18
Plate, 11″	25
Plate, chop, 12½″	35
Plate, chop, 14½″	40
Plate, party, 8″(nc)	6
Platter, Casual, 13¾″	40
Platter, oval, 14¾″	40
Sauce boat	25
Saucer	5
Saucer, Jumbo	10
Saucer for mug	10
Server, center handle	10
Server, 2-tier	30
Server, 3-tier	35
Shaker	10
Sherbet	20
Sugar	15
Sugar, individual	12
Teapot	55
Teapot, individual	35–40
Tile, oct/sq/rd, 6″	15
Tray, bread	35
Tray, condiment	22
Tray, square, 7½″ (nc)	15

Fruit plate and mixing bowls.

FRUIT AND FLOWERS Designed by Kay Hackett. "That's based on decoupage. As if you took a seed catalog and cut out flowers and put them on like this and you could turn the plate in any direction and they'd all be balanced. And nothing overlaps. In designing, I tried never to have one color on top of another, but to just miss it or be apart from it so that you didn't have to paint half of a leaf out here and have to fill it in this way, but rather two strokes would do the whole thing. So that each one of these is a perfect little entity in itself but put together as decoupage."

The 2-cup mug will be found with straight sides or tapered sides.

Fruit and Flower relish tray, celery tray and restyled sugar and creamer.

Ash tray, fluted, 5″ (nc)	12
Bowl, salad, 10″	45
Bowl, salad, 12″	65
Bowl, soup, coupe, 7½″	20
Bowl, soup, lug, 5½″	15
Bowl, vegetable, divided	45
Bowl, vegetable, round, 8″	35
Butter dish	40
Casserole, 8″	65
Casserole, individual, stick	25
Casserole w/handle, 6″	25
Casserole w/handle, 8″	35
Coaster/Ash tray	15
Coffee pot, 4 cup	55
Coffee pot, 8 cup	65
Coffee warmer	20
Creamer	15
Cruet	35
Cup	13
Dish, cereal, 5½″	15
Dish, fruit, 5½″	15
Dish, pickle	25
Dish, relish	35
Egg cup	10
Gravy boat	25
Gravy boat stand	15
Mug, coffee, low	15
Mug, coffee, 2 cup	25
Pitcher, 6 ounce	15
Pitcher, ½ pint	18
Pitcher, 1 pint	25

Pitcher, 1 quart	35
Pitcher, 2 quart	60
Plate, 6″	9
Plate, 7″	12
Plate, 8″	15
Plate, 9″	12
Plate, 10″	18
Plate, 11″	35
Plate, chop, 12½″	35
Plate, chop, 14½″	45
Plate, grill (nc)	25
Plate, party, 8″ (nc)	7
Platter, Casual, 13¾″	45
Platter, oval, 14¾″	45
Sauce boat	25
Saucer	6
Saucer for mug	10
Server, center handle	15
Server, 2-tier	30
Server, 3-tier	40
Shaker	12
Sugar	18
Sugar, individual	15
Teapot	65
Tile, oct/rd, 6″	15
Tray, bread	40
Tray, condiment	25

Shoveler Duck   Blue Jays, pair

Quail   Magnolia Warbler   Key West Quail Dove, wings spread

Falcon

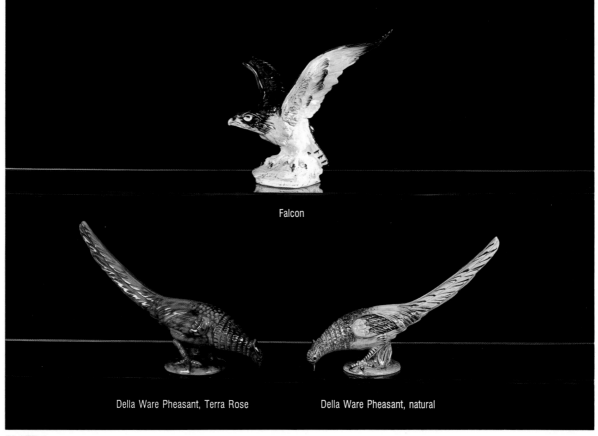

Della Ware Pheasant, Terra Rose   Della Ware Pheasant, natural

PLATE 1

Cockatoo, ivory w/yellow comb   Cockatoo, ivory w/green comb   Cockatoo, Terra Cotta

Porcelain Woodpecker   Dealer Sign

Wren , tan and brown   Parrakeets, blue   Parrakeets, green

Hen, yellow and gray   Coasters

PLATE 2

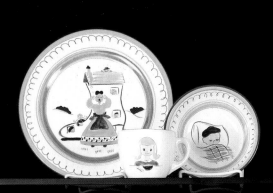

Woman in the Shoe (early)　　Pink Carousel tile　　Indian Campfire grill plate

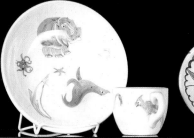

Wildlife bowl & cup　　Blue Bird divided dish　　Wizard of Oz cup & bowl

Musical Mugs

Jack & Jill　　Toy Soldiers　　Mary Had a
Little Lamb

Lamb feeding dish

Cat & the Fiddle cup & plate　　Hans/Fritz cup　　Mary Had
a Lamb cup
Lunning shape　　Flying Saucer plate and cup

PLATE 3

COUNTRY LIFE

Bowl, vegetable, 8"/Calf, chained

Bowl, vegetable, divided/Duck and ducklings

Plate, 10"/Farmer's wife harvesting carrots

Plate, 11"/Farmer baling hay

Plate, chop, 12½"/Farmhouse

Plate, chop, 14½"/Barn w/farm name

Dish, fruit, 5½"/Pony

Tray, bread/Hen with chicks

Plate, 8"/Cow standing in grass

Plate, 8"/Pig at fence

Casual Platter/Hen and ducklings

Soup, coupe, 8" Mallard w/dunking duck

Soup, coupe, 8"/Mallard

PLATE 4

#3148 Sand   #3253 Satin Blue   #3149 Marigold Yellow

#2017 Dusty Pink   #1958
Blue of the Sky   Deco vase,
Bronze Green   #1394 Rust

Rainbow Ware

Fish planter   Camel planter   Covered jar

#1388 dinner plates
Tangerine, Persian Yellow, Turquoise, Colonial Blue, Silver Green

PLATE 5

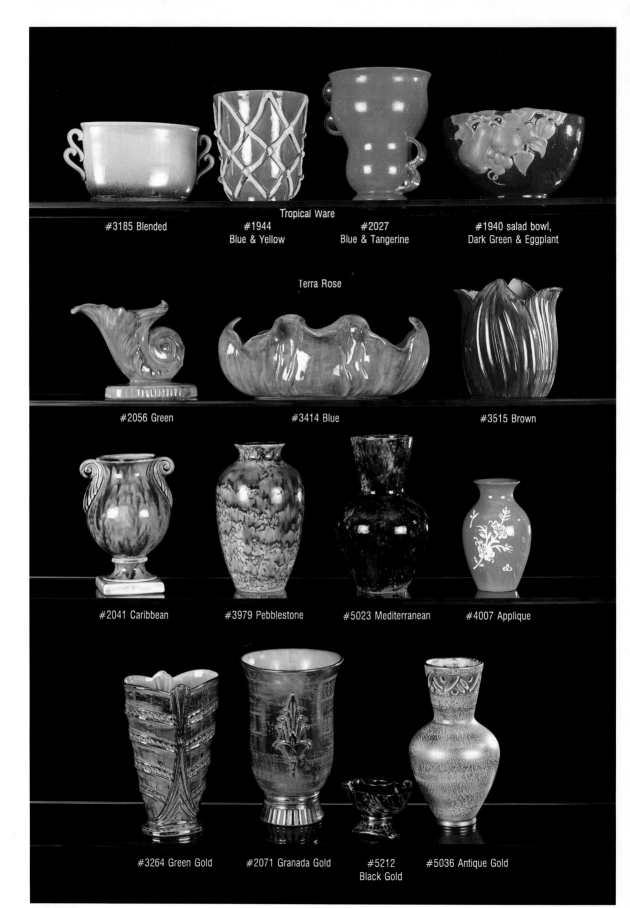

Tropical Ware

#3185 Blended

#1944
Blue & Yellow

#2027
Blue & Tangerine

#1940 salad bowl,
Dark Green & Eggplant

Terra Rose

#2056 Green

#3414 Blue

#3515 Brown

#2041 Caribbean

#3979 Pebblestone

#5023 Mediterranean

#4007 Applique

#3264 Green Gold

#2071 Granada Gold

#5212
Black Gold

#5036 Antique Gold

PLATE 6

#2000 Ranger carafe

#3511 Early Pennsylvania
Tulip, yellow

#3211 Early Pennsylvania
Tulip, blue

#1384 Bird ash tray

#1076B Early
Pennsylvania Tulip,
pink

Rabbit cotton holder

"Smoke"

Archie

Batch

Chief

Depression (Cry Baby)

Grand

Henpeck

Parson

Sport

PLATE 7

Buffalo   Calf   Colt   Draft Horse

Duck (Wild Duck)   Elephant   Giraffe   Gazelle

Goat   Rabbit   Sitting Dog   Wire-Haired Terrier

PLATE 8

GARDEN FLOWER Designed by Kay Hackett. The following flowers were used for the decoration: blue Balloon Flower, pink Bleeding Hearts, purple Campanula, yellow Calendula, blue Flax, blue Morning Glory, pink Phlox, pink Rose, yellow Sunflower and yellow Tiger Lily. So you will know what to look for, I've included the particular flower for each piece with the individual listing.

Bowl, salad, round, 10″/Campanula	40
Bowl, salad, round, 11″/Balloon Flower	45
Bowl, soup, lug, 5½″/Morning Glory	15
Bowl, vegetable, divided, round, 10″/Balloon Flower	40
Bowl, vegetable, round, 8″/Phlox	35
Casserole, 6″/Balloon Flower	22
Casserole, 8″/Balloon Flower	55
Casserole, w/handle, 6″/Balloon Flower	20
Casserole, w/handle, 8″/Tiger Lily	25
Cigarette box/Rose	30
Coaster/Ash tray/Rose	12
Creamer /Calendula & Morning Glory	10
Creamer, individual/Rose	12
Cup/Rose	10
Dish, cereal, 5½″/Morning Glory	15
Dish, fruit, 5½″/Calendula	12
Egg Cup/Campanula	10
Pitcher, ½ pint/Campanula	15
Pitcher, 1 pint /Rose	20
Pitcher, 1 quart/Balloon Flower	25
Pitcher, 2 quart/Sunflower	40
Plate, 6″/Balloon Flower	6
Plate, 8″/Bleeding Heart	12
Plate, 9″/Tiger Lily	12
Plate, 10″/Rose	15
Plate, 11″/Sunflower	22
Plate, chop, 12½″/Rose, Tiger Lily & Balloon Flower	35
Plate, chop, 14½″/Morning Glory & Sunflower	40
Saucer/Leaves	5
Server, center handle	10
Server, 2-tier	25
Server, 3-tier	35
Shaker, coupe or cylinder /Flax	8
Sherbet/Flax	20
Sugar/Calendula & Morning Glory	12
Sugar, individual/Bleeding Hearts	12
Teapot/Sunflower	45
Teapot, individual/Balloon Flower	35

Garden Flower stick handle casserole (frypan/skillet) and individual teapot.

GARLAND Designed by Kay Hackett. ". . . delicate green, wine-red beauty on soft gray background." KH: "That was influenced by decals, trying to do something small and delicate. We'd done big, bold things."

Bowl, salad, 10″	35
Bowl, salad, 12″	40
Bowl, soup, coupe, 7½″	20
Bowl, soup, lug, 5½″	15
Bowl, vegetable, divided	40
Bowl, vegetable, round, 8″	30
Butter dish	35
Casserole, 8″	50
Casserole, individual, stick	25
Casserole w/handle, 6″	20
Casserole w/handle, 8″	35
Cigarette Box, 3¾″ x 4½″	40
Coaster/Ash tray	12
Coffee pot, 8 cup	45
Coffee warmer	20
Creamer	10
Cruet	35
Cup	12
Dish, cereal, 5½″	15
Dish, fruit, 5½″	12
Dish, pickle	22
Dish, relish	25
Egg cup	12
Gravy boat	20
Gravy boat stand	12
Mug, coffee, 2 cup	25
Pitcher, 6 ounce	15
Pitcher, ½ pint	20
Pitcher, 1 pint	25
Pitcher, 1 quart	30
Pitcher, 2 quart	45
Plate, 6″	6
Plate, 8″	12
Plate, 9″	12
Plate, 10″	15
Plate, 11″	25
Plate, chop, 12½″	30
Plate, chop, 14½″	40
Platter, Casual, 13¾″	45
Saucer	5
Server, center handle	10
Server, 3-tier	35
Shaker	8
Sugar	15
Teapot	45
Tray, bread	35

Garland 8″ casserole and plate.

LYRIC Designed by Kay Hackett. "Black on white, laced with arabesques of mellow brown." KH: "My youngsters were in school in the fifties and they came home and made drawings of all-over curving lines intersecting, and filled in spaces. Non-objective art for third graders. I realized that you saw this on the counters in diners, and on textiles, etc., and I thought, Let's make a pattern. So all it amounted to was developing a series of lines and spaces that could be balanced and used on this very modern form." This was a sophisticated rendering of an otherwise simple drawing style.

Bowl, salad, 10″	35
Bowl, soup, lug, 5½″	12
Bowl, vegetable, divided	35
Bowl, vegetable, round, 8″	30
Casserole, individual, knob, 4″	18
Cigarette Box, 3¾″ x 4½″	35
Coaster/Ash tray	15
Coffee server	65
Creamer	14
Creamer, Casual	20
Cup	10
Mug, coffee, low	15
Mug, coffee, 2 cup	25
Plate, 6″	7
Plate, 8″	12
Plate, 10″	16
Plate, chop, 12½″	35
Saucer	4
Sugar	18
Sugar, Casual	20

Lyric flyer showing Casual sugar, creamer and coffee server.

MAGNOLIA Designed by Kay Hackett. " . . . striking tones of off-rose and white against a soft gray-green." KH: "That they told me was the hit of the ceramics show that year. We had done that because Mr. Stangl wanted to develop something where he could ask more.

"We were getting like two dollars a plate and he wanted to be able to ask three, and one of the things we could do was say it cost more to put this engobe on. And the lab did a lot of experimenting with me and I found that this white, you'd load the brush up till it almost dripped and then you'd skate it around in an area like this and end up with the whole surface shiny so it wouldn't have any streaks in it. What you could do with this white, you could skate the thing full or just touch it and make a drop. So with Magnolia there's areas where they skated it full or the little flowers in the background. That went very well for quite a while."

Pricing. Use these prices for Golden Harvest.

Golden Harvest condiment set; Magnolia #2000 carafe and plate.

Ash tray, rectangular	20
Bowl, salad, 10″	35
Bowl, salad, 12″	40
Bowl, soup, coupe, 7½″	20
Bowl, soup, lug, 5½″	12
Bowl, vegetable, covered, 8″	40
Bowl, vegetable, divided	35
Bowl, vegetable, round, 8″	25
Butter dish	35
Carafe/Vase	ND
Casserole, 6″	20
Casserole, 8″	40
Casserole, individual, knob	10
Casserole w/handle, 6″	20
Casserole w/handle, 8″	35
Cigarette Box, 3¾″ x 4½″	30
Coaster/Ash tray	12
Coffee pot, individual	50
Coffee pot, 8 cup	45
Coffee server	60
Coffee warmer	20
Creamer	7
Creamer, individual	12
Cruet	30

Cup	7
Dish, cereal, 5½″	12
Dish, fruit, 5½″	12
Dish, pickle	15
Dish, relish	18
Egg cup	10
Gravy boat	15
Gravy boat stand	10
Mug, coffee, 2 cup	25
Mug, coffee, low	15
Pitcher, 6 ounce	12
Pitcher, ½ pint	15
Pitcher, 1 pint	20
Pitcher, 1 quart	30
Pitcher, 2 quart	35
Plate, 6″	6
Plate, 8″	12
Plate, 9″	10
Plate, 10″	12
Plate, 11″	20
Plate, chop, 12½″	25
Plate, chop, 14½″	35
Platter, Casual, 13¾″	30
Saucer	4
Server, center handle	8
Shaker	8
Sugar	12
Sugar, individual	12
Teapot	50
Tray, bread	25
Tray, condiment	20

MOUNTAIN LAUREL

Bowl, salad, 10″	30	Egg cup	10
Bowl, salad, 11″	35	Pitcher, ½ pint	15
Bowl, soup, lug, 5½″	12	Pitcher, 1 pint	20
Bowl, vegetable, divided, round, 10″	30	Pitcher, 1 quart	25
Bowl, vegetable, round, 8″	25	Pitcher, 2 quart	35
Casserole, 6″	15	Plate, 6″	6
Casserole, 8″	50	Plate, 8″	10
Casserole w/handle, 6″	20	Plate, 9″	12
Casserole w/handle, 8″	30	Plate, 10″	15
Cigarette box	35	Plate, 11″	20
Coaster/Ash tray	12	Plate, chop, 12½″	30
Coffee pot, individual	35	Plate, chop, 14½″	40
Creamer	7	Saucer	4
Creamer, individual	12	Server, center handle	8
Cup	8	Shaker, coupe or cylinder	8
Dish, cereal, 5½″	12	Sherbet	20
Dish, fruit, 5½″	12	Sugar	12
		Sugar, individual	12
		Teapot	45

Mountain Laurel round divided vegetable and teapot.

PIE CRUST/SUNSHINE A short set with a ruffled rim. This shape will also be found in the three Terra Rose colors. Irene Sarnecki: "Piecrust was all hand cast. It was not jiggered. The fluted edge made it very susceptible to chipping."

Bowl, salad, 10″	30
Bowl, vegetable, round, 8″	20
Creamer	7
Cup	8
Dish, soup/cereal, 5½″	9
Footed compote	20
Plate, 6″	5
Plate, 8″	10
Plate, 10″	12
Plate, chop, 12½″	22
Saucer	3
Server, center handle	5
Sugar	12

Pie Crust cup, saucer and plate.

ROOSTER The shakers are undecorated. The rooster is similar to the one on Country Life — don't confuse the two.

Bowl, salad, 10″	45
Bowl, soup, coupe, 7½″	22
Bowl, soup, lug, 5½″	18
Bowl, vegetable, round, 8″	35
Cake stand	25
Clock	50
Creamer	12
Cup	12
Dish, fruit, 5½″	15
Dish, cereal, 5½″	15
Egg cup	15
Mug, coffee, 2 cup	25
Pitcher, 1 pint	25
Pitcher, 1 quart	35
Pitcher, 2 quart	45
Plate, 6″	8
Plate, 8″	12
Plate, 10″	22
Plate, chop, 12½″	35

Rooster plate, creamer, sugar, mug, shaker and jug, all in the revised rim shape.

Saucer	6
Server, center handle	15
Server, 2-tier	25
Server, 3-tier	35
Shaker	8
Sugar	15

STAR FLOWER Designed by Kay Hackett. "That's based on Christmas Rose, blooms in the south."

Ash tray, rectangular	20
Bowl, salad, 10″	40
Bowl, salad, 12″	50
Bowl, soup, lug, 5½″	12
Bowl, vegetable, covered, 8″	50
Bowl, vegetable, divided	35
Bowl, vegetable, round, 8″	35
Butter dish	35
Casserole, individual, knob	10
Cigarette box	30
Coaster/Ash tray	12
Coffee pot, individual	50
Coffee pot, 8 cup	45
Coffee warmer	18
Creamer	8
Creamer, individual	12
Cup	10
Dish, cereal, 5½″	12
Dish, fruit, 5½″	12
Dish, relish	25
Egg cup	10
Gravy boat	20
Gravy boat stand	12
Plate, 6″	6
Plate, 8″	10
Plate, 9″	10
Plate, 10″	13
Plate, chop, 12½″	30
Plate, chop, 14½″	35
Saucer	5
Server, center handle	8
Shaker	8
Sugar	12
Sugar, individual	12
Teapot	45

Star Flower plate and butter dish.

THISTLE Designed by Kay Hackett. This pattern was developed while J. M. Stangl was out of the country. Dave Thomas: "The Thistle pattern was one of the more successful single patterns made. He [Martin Stangl] had nothing to do with it. He was away on a three-month trip, came back, and we had already designed it, we had finished the thing up, we had photographed it, we had samples out to stores, it was a going fact. It couldn't be brought back.

"And he [Stangl] didn't like it. And the reason he didn't like it, cause he had a farm up here in Hunterdon County, and if you know what thistles do to cows when they're in a field, it gets in their hair, and he didn't like it. But when the sales started to soar, he said nothing."

Kay Hackett: "The thistle blossom was done with a twist of purple, one stroke, and another brush, a twist of pink; you had to spin it in your fingers so it would end up here. Then you took another brush with water and you went whoosh around the outside, so that these three strokes would give you the whole blossom. You didn't have to turn the plate or anything."

Note: A Japanese imitation, with a decal and no carving, was made. It is marked "Japan."

Thistle Chip 'n' Dip plate and three coffee pots: individual, 4-cup and 8-cup.

Ash tray, rectangular	25
Bowl, mixing, 4″ (nc)	12
Bowl, mixing, 5½″ (nc)	20
Bowl, mixing, 7″ (nc)	25
Bowl, mixing, 9″ (nc)	35
Bowl, salad, 10″	40
Bowl, salad, 12″	45
Bowl, soup, coupe, 7½″	20
Bowl, soup, lug, 5½″	15
Bowl, vegetable, covered, 8″	60
Bowl, vegetable, divided	35
Bowl, vegetable, round, 8″	30
Butter dish	35
Casserole, 6″	25
Casserole, 8″	60
Casserole, individual, knob	12
Casserole, individual, stick	25
Casserole w/handle, 6″	20
Casserole w/handle, 8″	30
Chip 'n' Dip (nc)	55
Cigarette Box	35

Coaster/Ash tray	12
Coffee pot, individual	50
Coffee pot, 4 cup	50
Coffee pot, 8 cup	45
Coffee server	60
Coffee warmer	20
Creamer	8
Creamer, individual	15
Cruet	30
Cup	7
Dish, cereal, 5½″	15
Dish, fruit, 5½″	12
Dish, pickle	20
Dish, relish	18
Egg cup	12
Gravy boat	20
Gravy boat stand	12
Mug, coffee, low	18
Mug, coffee, 2 cup	25
Pitcher, 6 ounce	15
Pitcher, ½ pint	20
Pitcher, 1 pint	25
Pitcher, 1 quart	35
Pitcher, 2 quart	40
Plate, 6″	6
Plate, 8″	10
Plate, 9″	10
Plate, 10″	15
Plate, 11″	30
Plate, chop, 12½″	30
Plate, chop, 14½″	40

Plate, grill (nc)	25	Shaker	8
Plate, party, 8″ (nc)	6	Sugar	15
Platter, Casual, 13¾″	35	Sugar, individual	15
Platter, oval, 14¾″	40	Teapot	40
Sauce boat	20	Tray, bread	25
Saucer	4	Tray, condiment	22
Server, center handle	10		

TULIP/BLUE/YELLOW Designed by Kay Hackett. "Mr. Stangl took me down to a museum in Philly to show me the Pennsylvania Dutch stuff. I made some sketches and when I came home, made half a dozen samples and one of them was the Tulip." Tulip in blue was made only for Marshall Field in Chicago.

Bean Pot, two handles (nc)	50
Bowl, salad, 10"	35
Bowl, salad, 11"	40
Bowl, soup, coupe, 7½"	20
Bowl, soup, lug, 5½"	12
Bowl, vegetable, divided, oval, 8"	35
Bowl, vegetable, divided, round, 10"	35
Bowl, vegetable, round, 8"	30
Casserole, 6"	25
Casserole, 8"	45
Casserole w/handle, 6"	20
Casserole w/handle, 8"	30
Cigarette Box	30
Coaster/Ash tray	12
Coffee pot, individual	35
Coffee pot, 8 cup	50
Creamer	8
Creamer, individual	12
Cup	10
Dish, cereal, 5½"	12
Dish, fruit, 5½"	12
Egg cup	10
Gravy boat	25
Mug, coffee, 2 cup	25
Pitcher, ½ pint	15
Pitcher, 1 pint	20
Pitcher, 1 quart	25
Pitcher, 2 quart	35
Plate, 6"	6
Plate, 8"	10
Plate, 9"	12
Plate, 10"	15
Plate, 11"	20
Plate, chop, 12½"	30
Plate, chop, 14½"	40
Saucer	4
Server, center handle	10
Shaker	8
Sherbet	20
Sugar	12
Sugar, individual	12
Teapot	40

Tulip Blue/Tulip Yellow cylinder shakers, old cup, restyled cup and plate.

WILD ROSE Designed by Kay Hackett.
"Wild Rose stays in full bloom, always!"

Bowl, soup, coupe, 7½″	20
Bowl, soup, lug, 5½″	15
Bowl, salad, 10″	35
Bowl, salad, 12″	40
Bowl, vegetable, divided	35
Bowl, vegetable, round, 8″	30
Butter dish	35
Cake stand	25
Casserole, 8″	50
Casserole, individual, stick	25
Casserole w/handle, 6″	20
Casserole w/handle, 8″	25
Cigarette Box	35
Coaster/Ash tray	12
Coffee pot, 4 cup	50
Coffee pot, 8 cup	50
Coffee warmer	20
Creamer	10
Cruet	30
Cup	7
Dish, cereal, 5½″	15
Dish, fruit, 5½″	12
Dish, pickle	20
Dish, relish	18
Egg cup	10
Gravy boat	25
Gravy boat stand	12
Mug, coffee, low	20
Mug, coffee, 2 cup	25
Pepper mill	ND
Pitcher, 6 ounce	15
Pitcher, ½ pint	20
Pitcher, 1 pint	25
Pitcher, 1 quart	35
Pitcher, 2 quart	45
Plate, 6″	6
Plate, 8″	10
Plate, 9″	10

Wild Rose plate and pepper mill.

Plate, 10″	15
Plate, 11″	22
Plate, chop, 12½″	30
Plate, chop, 14½″	40
Platter, Casual, 13¾″	35
Saucer	5
Server, center handle	10
Server, 2-tier	25
Server, 3-tier	35
Shaker	10
Sugar	15
Sugar, individual	15
Teapot	50
Tray, bread	30
Tray, condiment	25

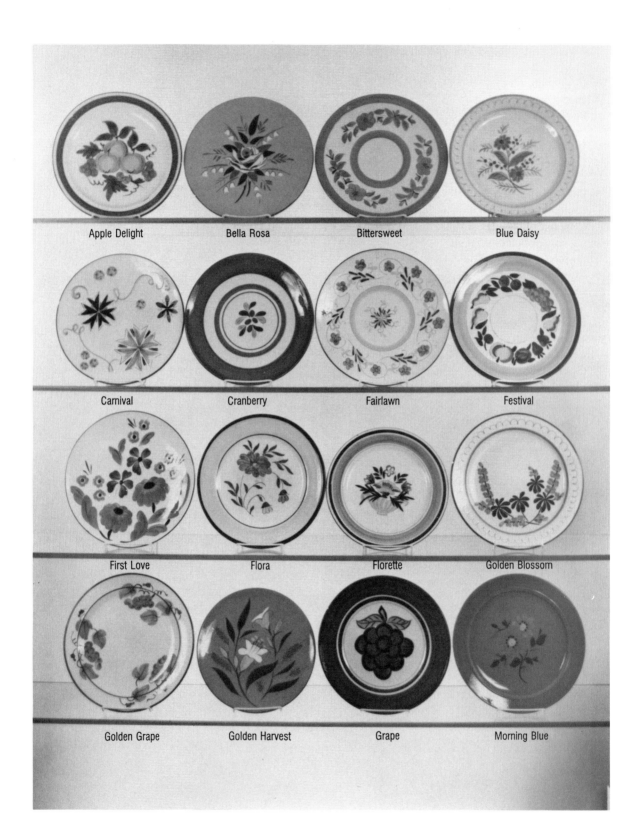

Apple Delight	Bella Rosa	Bittersweet	Blue Daisy
Carnival	Cranberry	Fairlawn	Festival
First Love	Flora	Florette	Golden Blossom
Golden Grape	Golden Harvest	Grape	Morning Blue

Orchard Song   Paisley   Petite Flowers   Pie Crust

Pink Lily   Prelude   Provincial   Ringles

Stardust   Tiger Lily   Water Lily   Willow

Windfall   Yellow Flower   Yellow Tulip

Dinnerware/Group List #1

Use this list for the following patterns: Apple Delight, Bachelor Button, Bella Rosa, Bittersweet, Blue Daisy, Cranberry, Fairlawn, Festival, First Love, Flora, Golden Blossom, Golden Grape, Grape, Jonquil, Mediterranean, Orchard Song, Prelude, Provincial, Sgraffito, Stardust, Tiger Lily, Water Lilies, Windfall and Yellow Tulip.

Ash tray, fluted	8
Bowl, salad, 10″	35
Bowl, salad, 12″	45
Bowl, soup, coupe, 7½″	12
Bowl, soup, flat, 8¼″	12
Bowl, soup, lug, 5½″	12
Bowl, vegetable, 8″	25
Bowl, vegetable, covered, 8″	35
Bowl, vegetable, divided	25–30
Butter, ¼ pound	35
Cake stand	20
Candle warmer	15
Casserole, 6″	15
Casserole, 8″	40
Casserole, individual, knob, 4″	10
Casserole, individual, stick-handle, 6″	15
Casserole, skillet, 6″	20
Casserole, skillet, 8″	25
Cigarette box	35
Coaster/Ash tray	8
Coffee pot, 8 cup	40
Creamer	8
Cruet	30
Cup	10
Dish, cereal, 5½″	12
Dish, fruit, 5½″	10
Egg cup	10
Gravy	15
Gravy liner	10
Mug, low	15
Mug, 2 cup	25
Pitcher, 6 ounce	15
Pitcher, ½ pint	20
Pitcher, 1 pint	25
Pitcher, 1 quart	35
Pitcher, 2 quart	40
Plate, 6″	5
Plate, 8″	10
Plate, 9″	12
Plate, 10″	15
Plate, 11″	10
Plate, chop, 12¼″	25
Plate, chop, 14½″	30
Plate, grill (steak), 11″ (nc)	15
Plate, picnic, 8″ (nc)	4
Plate, picnic, 10″ (nc)	5
Platter, Casual, 13¾″	35
Platter, oval, 14¾″	35
Sauce boat	20
Saucer	3
Server, center handle	7
Server, 2-tier	20
Server, 3-tier	25
Shaker	10
Sherbet	20
Sugar	12
Teapot, 6 cup	40
Tile	15
Tray, bread	25
Tray, pickle	15
Tray, relish	22

Dinnerware/Group List #2

Use this list for the following patterns: Aztec, Bamboo, Blue Melon, Colonial Silver, Florette, Galaxy, Monterey, Morning Blue, Paisley, Pink Lily, Posies, Ringles, Rustic, Scandinavia, Spun Gold, Terra Rose, Treasured, White Grape and Yellow Flower.

Item	Price
Bowl, salad, 10″	20
Bowl, salad, 12″	25
Bowl, soup, coupe, 7½″	10
Bowl, soup, flat, 8¼″	10
Bowl, soup, lug, 5½″	10
Bowl, vegetable, 8″	18
Bowl, vegetable, covered, 8″	30
Bowl, vegetable, divided	25–30
Butter, ¼ pound	25
Cake stand	20
Candle warmer	10
Casserole, 4″	12
Casserole, 6″	12
Casserole, 8″	30
Casserole, individual, knob, 4″	8
Casserole, individual, stick-handle, 6″	12
Casserole, skillet, 6″	12
Casserole, skillet, 8″	15
Cigarette box	25
Coaster/Ash tray	5
Coffee pot, 8 cup	35
Creamer	7
Cruet	20
Cup	10
Dish, cereal, 5½″	10
Dish, fruit, 5½″	10
Egg cup	8
Gravy	10
Gravy liner	6
Mug, stack	15
Mug, 2 cup	15
Pitcher, 6 ounce	10
Pitcher, ½ pint	15
Pitcher, 1 pint	20
Pitcher, 1 quart	25
Pitcher, 2 quart	35
Plate, 6″	5
Plate, 8″	9
Plate, 9″	10
Plate, 10″	12
Plate, chop, 12¼″	15
Plate, chop, 14½″	20
Platter, Casual, 13¾″	25
Platter, oval, 14¾″	25
Saucer	3
Server, center handle	5
Server, 2-tier	15
Server, 3-tier	20
Shaker	5
Sugar	12
Teapot, 6 cup	35
Tray, bread	20
Tray, pickle	12
Tray, relish	18

Prestige Line

Sculptured Ware

"A ceramic masterpiece created by skilled Stangl Artisans. Sculptured patterns emphasize the design and create depth and dimension that cannot be achieved on regular dinnerware." All these decorations are on the scalloped shape, with the exception of Blossom Ring and Inspiration, which are on the coupe shape. The Dogwood shape was modeled by Auguste Jacob.

Colonial Dogwood (fawn [beige] and white), Pink Dogwood (pink and white) and White Dogwood (white and green) are on the same shape as the Dogwood (pink and green) used for Della Ware. Dahlia (blue flowers, also called Blue Dahlia) and Pink Cosmos (pink flowers, also called Cosmos) are the same shape. Do not confuse with the hand-painted Cosmos on the #2000 shape. Sculptured Fruit (avocado green and yellow-gold) and Sierra (beige and brown) are the same shape. Blossom Ring (green and white) and Inspiration (multicolor and white with brushed gold over flowers) are the same shape. Inspiration has gold decoration but is included here because the assortment found is the same as the other sculptured lines. Dahlia may not be found in all pieces.

Pricing. The Dogwoods are at the top of the range, Sculptured Fruit in the middle, and Dahlia and Pink Cosmos at the bottom. Sierra is 50% of the low price. Use the gold-decorated prices below for Inspiration. Items found in one pattern only are listed with the pattern initials after a slash.

Bowl, footed, 8″	30
Bowl, footed, 10″	40
Bowl, salad, 10″	35
Bowl, soup, flat/SF	15
Bowl, soup, lug	12–15
Bowl, vegetable, 8″	25–30
Dish, cereal/SF	15
Dish, cereal/WD	20
Dish, fruit, 5½″/SF	12
Cake, footed	25
Clock	40–50
Creamer	7–10
Cup	10–12
Plate, 6″	5–6
Plate, 8″	8–10
Plate, 10″	12–15
Plate, chop, 12½″	25–30
Plate, chop, 14½″	30–35
Platter, oval, 14¾″	35
Saucer	4–5
Server, center handle	10
Server, 2-tier	30
Server, 3-tier	35
Shaker	10–12
Sugar	12–15
Tile, round, 6″/SF	15
Tile, square, 6″/WD	20

Gold-decorated line

These are Concord ("Fruit decoration in delft blue and satin gold"), Florentine (carved pattern on rim and in center of well, covered with gold and green), Frosted Fruit ("Satin gold on a soft green background, with swirl effect and fruit decoration"), and Red Ivy ("A border design of red leaves with orange tendrils and jewel-like accents of bright gold"). Wildwood (multicolor flowers on rim) does not appear in flyers but seems to be the same assortment as the others. Also, see Inspiration above.

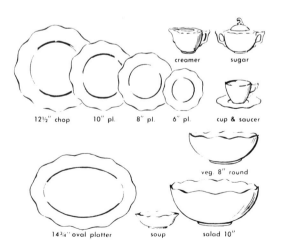

creamer sugar

12½″ chop 10″ pl. 8″ pl. 6″ pl. cup & saucer

veg. 8″ round

14¾″ oval platter soup salad 10″

The scalloped shape was used for all sculptured lines except Inspiration.

Florentine   Concord   Frosted Fruit

Dahlia   Inspiration   Red Ivy

Sculptured Fruit   Blossom Ring   Pink Dogwood

Kay Hackett: "Mr. Stangl said the reason those patterns were not more popular was because the matte glaze gives you a rough texture if you move your fork across. It goes 'zzzzzzzz' instead of just being slick. But I thought it gave my colors such a lovely soft feeling, it was like having a whole new palette to work with."

All patterns have the rim soup except Florentine, which has the coupe soup and vegetable bowl.

Bowl, salad, large	45
Bowl, soup, rim or coupe	12
Bowl, vegetable, 8″	25
Cigarette box	35
Coaster/Ash tray	12
Coffee pot	40
Creamer	7
Cup	10
Jug, 6 ounce	10
Jug, ½ pint	12
Jug, 1 pint	15
Plate, 6″	6
Plate, 8″	10
Plate, 10″	15
Plate, 11″	18
Plate, chop, 14½″	35
Saucer	3
Sugar	12
Teapot	35

Stoneware

Beginning in 1971, these patterns were produced on a "unique stoneware body Dura-fired for extra strength . . . oven safe . . . dishwasher safe."

Two shapes were used, the Contempo and the Croyden. An original flyer lists eight patterns: Antigua (Contempo), Delmar (Croyden), Diana (Contempo), Roxanne (Contempo), Rustic Garden (Contempo), Sesame (Croyden), Susan (Contempo), Trinidad (Croyden).

Other patterns known to be stoneware are: Adrian/IS (this was an Altman's exclusive; don't confuse with similarly named Della Ware pattern), Sun Pebbles (Contempo) which was also made on the coupe shape, Wood Rose (Croyden) and Yellow Tulip (Croyden) which was later made in the regular dinnerware line on the coupe shape.

The same items were made in both shapes. The casserole lids could be used as serving dishes. Some items had a plain color band only, no pattern; these are marked /P (for Plain) in the list below. Coupe items that will be found in Sun Pebbles only are marked /SP in the list below.

Pricing. Add 10% to the stoneware listings for Rustic Garden and Sun Pebbles.

Bowl, round, salad, 10″	20
Bowl, round, vegetable, 8″	18
Bowl, soup, flat/SP	8
Bowl, soup, lug/SP	8
Bowl, vegetable divided/SP	35
Cake, footed	18
Casserole, individual, 5½″/P	10
Casserole, 8″	25
Coffee carafe, 6 cup	25
Creamer/P	7
Cup/P	8
Dish, soup/cereal/P	8
Dish, fruit/dessert/P	6
Egg cup/P	8
Mug, stack/P	12
Pitcher, 6 ounce/SP	10
Pitcher, ½ pint/SP	15
Pitcher, 1 pint/SP	18
Pitcher, 1 quart/SP	20
Pitcher, 2 quart/SP	25
Plate, 6″	7
Plate, 8″	9
Plate, 10″	15
Plate, chop, 12½″	25
Saucer/P	3
Shaker/P	5
Sugar/P	10
Teapot, 6 cup	25
Tile, round, 6″/SP	12

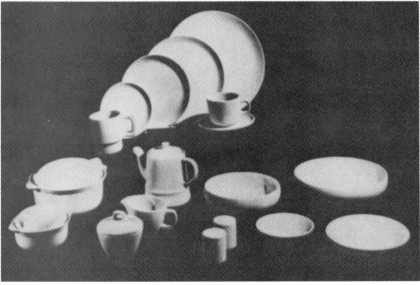

The Croyden shape.

Late Dinnerware

In Stangl's later years, several dinnerware lines were brought out that were a departure from the hand-painted patterns. Two of the most popular are listed here.

INDIAN SUMMER Designed by Roy Hamilton. Ovenproof dinnerware with underglaze decorations. Originally made for Tiffany and Company, New York City. It later went into national distribution.

"... this pottery has a country feeling in its primary colors of Sand (a buttery buff) and Earth (a warm milk-chocolate). There's a country look, too, in the primitive form and ridged texture, which imparts a hand-thrown quality that complements any decor."

The mug and the cup look the same, differing only in their capacity. The two salad bowls and the vegetable bowl make up a three-piece bowl set. A brunch set consisted of the mug, the 10½″ plate and the soup/cereal bowl.

Every piece was available in Plain Earth or Plain Sand. In addition, some Earth pieces were decorated with subtle tones of blue and dark blue or white and black. Those that were available decorated are marked with a /D.

Beverage server (coffee/teapot)	30
Bowl, salad, round, 3 quart, 10″	25
Bowl, salad, round, 5 quart, 12″	30
Bowl, vegetable, round, 2 quart, 8″	20
Bowl, soup/cereal, 15 ounce/D	12
Casserole, 3 quart	30
Casserole, 5½ quart	35
Creamer	8
Cup, 8 ounce/D	9
Jug, 24 ounce	18
Jug, 48 ounce	25
Mug, 14 ounce/D	12
Plate, high rim, 7″/D	6
Plate, high rim, 10½″/D	10
Plate, chop, high rim, 12″/D	18

Saucer/D	3
Sugar, open	8

MAIZE-WARE Designed and modeled by Rudy Kleinbeckel, from an idea of John Bonistall, Stangl vice-president, who had been president of Shawnee Pottery as well as Terrace Ceramics, both of which produced corn lines.

"Created for the gourmet who prefers oversized dinner plates, mugs, bowls, platters and other serving accessories in durable hand-crafted stoneware. The colorful glazes are fired over embossed corn kernels and leaves, making the ware ovenproof, alcohol-proof, acid-proof, dishwasher-safe, and husband-resistant. These are real decorative accessories for cookouts on the patio, at the beach, or anywhere that provender and potables, in generous portion, are served. An appreciated gift for the amateur chef, the playboy with culinary inclinations or a thoughtful addition to the party-pantry. Maize-Ware is the informal dinnerware that makes any meal an event!"

The sugar doubled as a grease bowl. A brunch set consisted of a brunch bowl, mug and 10″ plate.

Maize-Ware was made in four colors: Harvest-Yellow, Pioneer-Brown, Summer-Green and Winter-Tan.

Bowl, brunch, 7½″	12
Bowl, soup/cereal, 15 ounce	12
Bowl, vegetable, round, 8″	18
Butter, ¼ pound	25
Creamer	8
Cup	10
Mug, 16 ounce	15
Plate, 8¼″	10
Plate 10⅝″	15
Plate, chop, 12″	25
Saucer	3
Shaker, each	10
Sugar/grease bowl	18
Trivet, round, 7½″	15

048 LARGE PITCHER, 48 ounces. Available in PLAIN EARTH (shown above) or PLAIN SAND.

047 PITCHER, 24 ounces. Available in PLAIN EARTH (shown above) or PLAIN SAND.

006 HIGH-RIM CHOP PLATE, 12″ Diameter. Available hand-decorated or undecorated (shown above).

001 HIGH-RIM DINNER PLATE, 10½″ Diameter. Available hand-decorated or undecorated (shown above).

002 HIGH-RIM SALAD/DESSERT PLATE, 7″ Diameter. Available hand-decorated or undecorated (shown above).

033 LARGE CASSEROLE, 5½ quarts. Domed Cover. Available in PLAIN-SAND (shown above) or PLAIN-EARTH.

034 CASSEROLE, 3 quarts, domed cover. Available in PLAIN-SAND (shown above) or PLAIN-EARTH.

029 BEVERAGE SERVER, 40 ounces, domed cover. Available in PLAIN-EARTH (shown above) or PLAIN-SAND.

Stangl POTTERY ESTABLISHED IN 1805   P.O. Box 2080, Trenton, New Jersey 08607, (609) 695-8538

210 SUGAR AND CREAMER SET Shown above in Summer-Green. Individually cartoned. Consists of: 1—Creamer(208) and Covered Sugar Bowl(209)

215 COVERED BUTTER DISH Shown above in Pioneer-Brown. Holds quarter-pound stick. Available in standard pack.

AUTHENTIC EARLY-AMERICAN STONEWARE
DISHWASHER-SAFE
MAIZE-WARE®
STANGL POTTERY • Trenton, NJ 08607
Quality Since 1805
FOR MICROWAVE and CONVENTIONAL OVENS

225 5 PIECE SERVING SET Shown above in Harvest-Yellow. Individually cartoned. Consists of: 1—Large Chop Plate, 12"(206) • 1—Large Vegetable Bowl, 8"(207) • 1—Creamer(209) • 1—Covered Sugar Bowl(208)

ESTABLISHED 1805
Stangl
POTTERY

P.O. Box 2080, Trenton, New Jersey 08607, (609) 695-8538

230 3 PIECE BRUNCH SET Shown above in Summer-Green. Also shown on cover in Pioneer Brown. Individually cartoned. Consists of: 1—Large Dinner Plate, 10⅝"(201) • 1—Large Brunch Bowl, 7½"(211) • 1—16 oz. Beverage Mug(218)

235 12 PIECE BRUNCH SET Not shown. Individually cartoned. Consists of: 4—Large Dinner Plates, 10⅝"(201) • 4—Large Brunch Bowls, 7½" (211) • 4—16 oz. Beverage Mugs(218)

240 4 PIECE MUG SET Shown above in Harvest-Yellow. Individually cartoned. Consists of: 4—16 oz. Beverage Mugs(218)

245 12 PIECE MUG SET Not shown. Individually cartoned. Consists of: 12—16 oz. Beverage Mugs(218)

250 5 PIECE RANGE SET Shown above in Pioneer-Brown. Individually cartoned. Consists of: 1—Covered Grease Bowl(208) • 1—Large Round Trivet, 7½"(226) • 1—Salt and Pepper Set(227)

TOWN AND COUNTRY ". . . recaptures the flavor of the popular enamelware of the last century."

The butter bottom, gravy underplate and oval relish tray are all the same piece. The cake plate turns upside-down to become the Chip & Dip. The coffee mug is taller and narrower than the soup mug; the latter is the same as the juicer stand. The relish and the vanity tray are the same piece, and in some listings is also called an ash tray. The tureen was sold as a four-piece set (lid, bottom, ladle and chop plate). The sponge holder is the same as the soup/cereal. The cheese-and-cracker is shaped like a dust pan.

Town and Country is one color sponged over white engobe so that some white shows through. It was made in black, blue, brown, green, honey (added in 1977) and yellow. Crimson is listed in a 1974 catalog but has not been reported.

Pricing. Honey is about 10% less than the low price. Some items have only been seen in blue or yellow.

	Blue	Other Colors
Baking dish, rectangular, tab handles, 1½ quart, 7″ x 10″	60	40
Baking dish, rectangular, tab handles, 2½ quart, 9″ x 14″	85	60
Bean pot/cookie jar, 3 quart	85	65
Bowl, chowder/chili, 26 ounce, 6¾″	30	25
Bowl, fruit, 2½ quart, 10″	55	45
Bowl, pear shape, 8″	–	25
Bowl, porridge, 26 ounce, 6½″	40	25
Bowl, salad, round, 3 quart, 10″	55	40
Bowl, soup/cereal, 15 ounce, 5¾″	25	20
Bowl, vegetable, round, 1½ quart, 8″	45	35
Butter, ¼ pound	45	35
Cake plate/Chip & Dip, 12½″	85	60
Candleholder, flower shape, pair, 2¼″ high	45	–
Candleholder w/finger ring (glass globe)	45	35
Candlestick, pair, 7½″	85	50
Candy, clover shape, 3 part	40	–
Canister, milk pail shape, 3 quart	85	60
Casserole, 1½ quart	60	45
Casserole, 2 quart	60	45
Casserole, 2½ quart	65	50
Casserole, 3 quart	65	50
Cheese & cracker (dust pan shape)	75	60
Clock, plate, 10″	–	45
Clock, skillet shape (battery powered)	65	55
Coffee pot, 5 cup	75	50
Cornucopia, 10½″	–	55
Creamer	20	15
Cup	18	12
Dessert mold, fluted, 6″	40	35
Dessert mold, ribbed, 7½″	45	40
Gravy boat	30	25
Gravy boat stand	20	15
Pitcher, 1½ pint	40	35
Pitcher, 2½ pint	50	45
Pitcher, 2½ quart	75	65
Juicer, citrus, on stand	60	50
Ladle	40	25
Lamp	150	–
Mug, coffee, 13 ounce	35	25
Mug, soup, 14 ounce	35	25
Napkin ring	15	8
Pan, bread/loaf, 2 quart, 4¾″ x 10″	50	35
Pie baker, 10½″	45	35
Plate, 6″	9	6
Plate, 8″ (8¼″)	20	12
Plate, 10″ (10⅝″)	25	15
Plate, chop, 12½″	40	30
Platter, oval, 11″	50	25
Platter, oval, 15″	60	35
Relish tray, square, 7½″	25	20
Saucer	8	4
Shaker, cylinder shape	12	10
Shaker, cylinder shape, handled	15	12
Snack server, skillet shape, 8½″	50	30
Spoon rest, 8¾″	35	25
Sugar	30	25
Teapot, 5 cup	75	50
Tidbit, single, 10″	30	15
Tile, square, 6″	20	15

Tray, snack, oval, 8¼	20	15		Flower pot/planter, 5″	40	20
Tureen, 3½ quart	225	150		Flower pot/planter, 7″	50	25
Wall pocket, 7½″ long x 4⅜″ tall	50	—		Ginger jar	85	50
				Pitcher & bowl set, small	175	100
				Pitcher & bowl set, large	225	150
Bath Accessories				Shaving mug	40	20
				Soap dish, rectangular	40	35
Ash tray, bathtub shape	40	25		Sponge bowl, round	25	20
Canister, corked	50	35		Tissue box cover	50	35
Chamberpot, handled	85	65		Toothbrush holder	45	35
Flower pot/planter, 3″	20	10		Tumbler, 9 ounce	25	20
Flower pot/planter, 4″	30	15		Vanity tray, square	25	20

Town & Country

DINNERWARE, SERVING PIECES AND ACCESSORIES

All items available in all colors. Blue, Brown, Yellow, Green, and *NEW* for 1977 — Honey, featured on this page . . . Mix and match to suit your fancy.

Stangl has recaptured the charm and beauty of a past century with their authentic and faithful recreation of early enamelware.

Each and every piece of Town & Country is hand decorated to create that one-of-a-kind look unique to Stangl.

Reproduced in Stangl's resilient double-fired body. Every item is dishwasher safe and perfect for oven-to-table use, even the latest microwave ovens.

The complete line of Town & Country Dinnerware   20 piece set 020   5 piece set 025

Please use the 5-digit item numbers when ordering. First 2-digits indicate color. See list below. Last 3-digits indicate specific shape or set.

Specify:

Blue 10	Honey 13
Brown 11	Yellow 14
Green 12	

Example, 10-001 is Town & Country dinner plate in blue. All items come in all colors.

A. Chop Plate, 12" 006	J. Butter Dish, Covered 015	R. Casserole, Covered, 2 qt. . . 034
B. Coffeepot, 5-cup 016	K. Plate, Dinner, 10⅜" 001	S. Sugar Bowl, Covered 008
C. Teapot, 5-cup 029	L. Cup, 8 oz. 004	T. Creamer 009
D. Gravy/Stand 017	M. Saucer, 6" 005	U. Dessert Mold, Ribbed, 7½" 040
E. Oval Platter, 15" 022	N. Bowl, Soup/Cereal, 5¾",	V. Dessert Mold, Fluted, 6" . . 039
F. Pitcher 2½ qt. 048	15 oz. 003	W. Plate, Bread & Butter, 6" . . 021
G. Candlesticks (pair) 7½" . . . 036	O. Plate, Salad, 8¼" 002	X. Napkin Rings (set of 4) . . . 044
H. Salt & Pepper (handled) . . . 028	P. Skillet Snack Server, 8½" . . 050	Y. Baking Dish, 1½ qt. 030
I. Bowl, Vegetable, 8", 1½ qt. 007	Q. Casserole, Covered, 3 qt. . . 033	

Sizes and capacities are approximate

The complete line of Town & Country Dinnerware   20 piece set . . . . . . 020 5 piece set 025

AA. Salt & Pepper 027	JJ. Bowl, Fruit, 10", 2½ qt. . 012	QQ. Pitcher, 1½ pt. 046
BB. Oval Snack Tray, 8¼" . . . 024	KK. Skillet Clock, Battery	RR. Bowl, Porridge, 6½",
CC. Relish/Vanity Tray, 7½" . 026	Powered 049	26 oz. 013
DD. Cannister, Milk Pail, 3 qt. . 038	LL. Loaf Pan, 2 qt. 043	SS. Candleholder/Globe 037
EE. Oval Platter, 11¾" 023	MM. Mug, Soup, 14 oz. 019	TT. Chip & Dip/Cake Plate . . 035
FF. Spoon Rest, 8¼" 051	NN. Tureen, Soup, 4-piece,	UU. Baking Dish, 2½ qt. 031
GG. Bean Pot/Cookie Jar, 3 qt. 032	3½ qt. 052	VV. Pie Plate, 11" 045
HH. Bowl, Salad, 10", 3 qt. . . 014	OO. Ladle 042	WW. Mug, Coffee, 13 oz. 018
II. Bowl, Chowder/Chili,	PP. Juicer, Citrus/Stand 041	XX. Pitcher, 2½ pt. 047
6¾", 26 oz. 010		

20 Piece Starter Set
4 - Dinner Plates 4 - Soup/Cereal Bowls
4 - Salad Plates 4 - Cups & Saucers

5 Piece Service Set
1 - Chop Plate, 1 - Vegetable Bowl
1 - Sugar Bowl & Cover 1 - Creamer

Sizes and capacities are approximate

FLEMINGTON OUTLET

Dave Thomas: "We tried to reclaim when possible. Particularly birds, we would reglaze a bird. Or touch up, but generally no, it was such a lucrative market in Flemington, such a lucrative market."

Throughout the period of my research, I heard conflicting reports as to whether anything was done exclusively for the Flemington outlet. The answer is more complicated than a simple"yes" or "no."

Dave Thomas: "We were constantly experimenting with different bodies, glazes, colors, techniques of application: spray, brush, whatnot, stipple; then we would pass [the samples] through our committee. If we could see something that looked favorable or encouraging, we'd move on it but most of the time the stuff got put in a box: 'Send it to Flemington,' that got to be the byword."

Irene Sarnecki: "Sometimes, like I said, he would make so many of these and maybe send them up to Flemington to see how they would

Antique Rose seems to have been a pattern made only for Flemington.

Postcard showing interior of Flemington outlet, with sample plates and lamps surrounding an old bottle kiln.

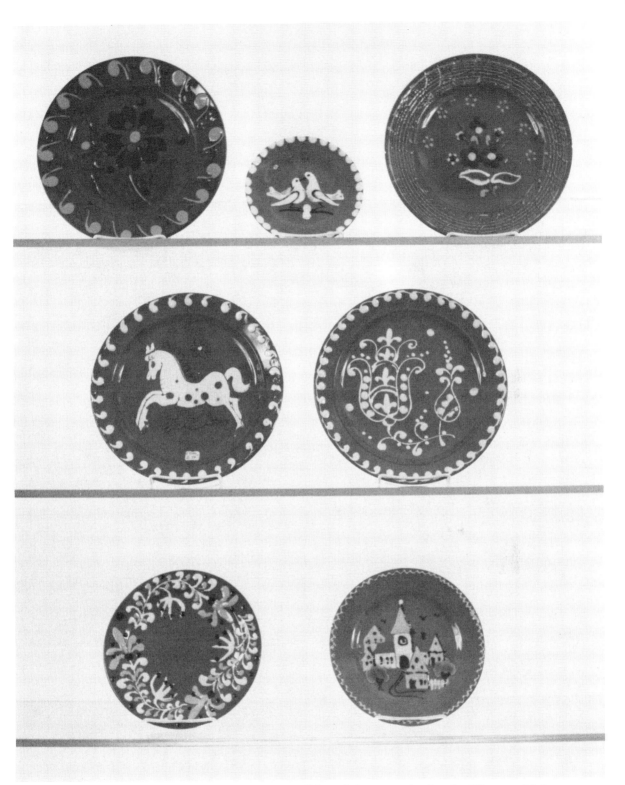

Gingerbread was made in a wide variety of motifs, some just slight variations on each other; the difference might be in the rim treatment only.

go, and then maybe we'd put it in the line. He would use that as a testing place."

Dave Thomas: "That's right, Flemington was the trial area."

Potential dinnerware patterns would be displayed and customers were asked to vote for their favorite.

GINGERBREAD   These were all done, apparently, by Rose Herbeck who signed her pieces with her initials in reverse—HR. They are slip decorated and covered with a clear glaze. Although made in Trenton, these seem to have been sold only at the outlet.

Pricing. For a 9″ plate with floral or abstract decoration, $40–50. Add 50% for birds, houses and other unusual decorations.

SECONDS   Lots of seconds were given inexpensive treatment and sent down to Flemington. Kay Hackett: "Things that had been carved and when they came out of the kiln they were defective, they were twisted, they had chips, something was wrong, and they would send them into decorating and tell a girl to paint them with French green, and all day long she'd paint the leaves, the flowers, the bands in French green, sometimes even the whole plate, and [we'd] send them to Flemington and get

something out of it." Solid colors, Terra Rose and other treatments will be found. See also my comments in the Preface.

SPECIALTY ITEMS   Rose Herbeck, in addition to the Gingerbread, seems to have been responsible for Wedding and Anniversary plates (which were displayed at the outlet and orders were taken) and other special items.

This Sunburst plate is an "HR" special.

FLOWER POTS AND PLANTERS

Stangl made a number of flowerpots, but the most popular are the hand-decorated ones in the three shapes covered below.

The one called a planter looks like a traditional rimmed flower pot. The two other shapes are called cache pots; one looks like a pail and the other is bowl shaped.

Note: For Caughley and for Town and Country flower pots, see those respective listings.

BOWL-SHAPE CACHE POTS Decorations include Rosebud, Trees (thick and thin brown vertical lines) and Violet.

	Trees	Flowers
6½″	25	30
8″	30	35
9″	35	40

PAIL-SHAPE CACHE POTS Decorations include Bamboo, Butterflies and Posies (same as the dinnerware).

6½″	30
8″	35
9″	40

PLANTERS The flower pot shape comes in a wide variety of decorations, including Town and Country (blue, brown, green, honey or yellow), Stripes (blue, mustard, olive or red), and the following florals: Blue Flower, Golden Iris, Pine Cone, Red Rose, Sun Flower, Violet, Wild Golden Rose and Yellow Tulip. The stripes are either horizontal around the bottom with a white rim, or vertical on the rim with a white bottom.

	Stripes	Flowers
3″	5	10
4″	10	15
5″	15	20
7″	25	30

Top left: *Town and Country.* Group at top right, reading top to bottom: *Pine Cone, Sun Flower, Yellow Tulip, Blue Flower, Golden Iris, Violet, and Red Rose.* Bottom left: *Stripes in Mustard, Olive, Red, Blue.* Bottom right: *Wild Golden Rose in four different sizes.*

GIFTWARE

Early Giftware

The items designated as "early" in this section were made in the thirties and into the forties.

There are many colors listed for these pieces: Blue of the Sky, Bronze Green, Champagne, Colonial Blue, Dusty Pink, Green Matte, Ivory Antique, Marigold Yellow, Ocher, Oyster White, Rust, Persian Yellow, Sand, Satin Blue, Satin Brown, Satin Green, Satin White, Satin Yellow, Silver Green, Surf White, Tangerine and Twilight Blue.

Many of these colors have been difficult to identify. It is thought that some of them may have had their names changed. Possibly Green Matte became Satin Green, and Surf White seems to have become Satin White; there may be others. If names were changed, we don't know if there were formula changes as well. Other colors may differ only in the overglaze used: glossy or matte.

Compounding the problem are the variations in each color. If you look at the Colonial Blue or the Silver Green on the Colonial dinnerware, you can see wide color variations.

For each line, I have listed the colors found in company literature; other colors may be found.

A number of these pieces were later used for the gold- and silver-decorated lines, though sometimes the numbers were changed.

ANIMAL FIGURES (1940) The figures were hand decorated in natural colors, with the exception of the 5″ elephant. Records indicate that all animals except the Calf, Colt, Goat and Sitting Dog were available in Antique Ivory Crackled and Turquoise Blue Crackled.

The small animals were available originally for sixty cents apiece. The Calf, Colt, Goat and Sitting Dog were originally priced at $1.50.

Mystery. Animals first appear in Stangl records dated January, 1940, and include a "Wild Duck" #3250, 3¼″ high. It looks like the Standing Duck but it has an upturned tail, though the drawings are not always reliable. The birds first appear in May, 1940, and show a "Duck" #3281, 4″ high. The tail is unclear. The one in the color section in this book was brought home in 1940, along with other animals, by a plant employee. It is 4″ high and has an upturned tail. If it's a #3250, why is it 4″ high? If it's a #3281, why is it as scarce as the animals and not as plentiful as the other ducks? For now, I have listed it with the animals as #3281.

Buffalo, 2½″/3246	200
Antique Ivory Crackled	50–75
Granada Gold	50–75
Turquoise Blue Crackled	50–75
Calf, 3½″/3279	125
Colt, 5″/3277	300
Marbleized	50–75
Dog, sitting, 5¼″/3280	
Brown w/black spots	125
Granada Gold	50–75
White w/black spots	125
Dog, Wire-Haired Terrier, 3¼″/3243	300
Antique Ivory Crackled	50–75
Turquoise Blue Crackled	50–75
Draft Horse, 3″/3244	125
Antique Ivory Crackled	50–75
Marbleized	50–75
Turquoise Blue Crackled	50–75
Duck, 4″/3281	125
Antique Ivory Crackled	50–75
Turquoise Blue Crackled	50–75
Elephant, 3″/3249	125+
Antique Ivory Crackled	50–75
Turquoise Blue Crackled	50–75
Elephant, 5″	
Granada Gold/Solid Black/Solid Gold	50–75
Gazelle, 3¾″/3247	125
Antique Ivory Crackled	50–75
Turquoise Blue Crackled	50–75

Bird on Ash Tray/1323

Bird-shaped Ash
Tray /3210

Bird Flower Pot/1778

Scottie Flower Pot/1775

Gazelle Candle
Holder/1321

Gazelle Insert
(Flower Frog)/1320

Pig Ash Tray/1745

Pig Bank/1076B

Pig Cactus Pot/1076C

Rabbit Flower Pot/1917

Swan Flower Pot/1394

Giraffe, 2½"/3248	150
Antique Ivory Crackled	50–75
Turquoise Blue Crackled	50–75
Goat, 5"/3278	300
Rabbit, 2"/3245	125
Antique Ivory Crackled	50–75
Turquoise Blue Crackled	50–75

ANIMAL WARE The bird, pig, Scottie and swan items date to at least 1935. The catalog lists solid colors of Blue of the Sky, Colonial Blue, Dusty Pink, Green Matte, Rust, Satin Blue, Satin White, Silver Green, Surf White, Tangerine and Yellow. Not all pieces were made in all colors.

See also Miniatures and Rainbow Ware below.

Bird Ash tray, hexagonal/1384	100–150
Bird on Ash Tray, 5"/1323	100–150
Bird-shaped Ash Tray/3210	ND
Bird Flower Pot, 6½"/1778	ND
Dog, Scottie Flower Pot, 7"/1775	100–150
Gazelle Candle Holder, 6"/1321	100–150
Gazelle Insert (Flower Frog), 6"/1320	100–150
Pig Ash Tray, 3"/1745	
Solid colors	50
Pig Bank, 4"/1076B	
Hand Decorated	125
Solid colors	75–100
Pig Cactus Pot, 4"/1076C	
Hand Decorated	75–100
Solid colors	50
Rabbit Cotton Holder	
Hand Decorated	ND
Solid colors	ND
Rabbit Flower Pot, 9"/1917	100–150
Swan Flower Pot, 4"/1394–4"	15–25
Swan Flower Pot, 6"/1394–6"	25–35
Swan Flower Pot, 9"/1394–9"	35–50
Swan Flower Pot, 13"/1394–13"	50–75

BLENDED COLORS (ca 1940) These pieces appear briefly in old catalog sheets under drawings of what is described as "Hand Decorated" ware. They appear to be hand sprayed. They are listed as being available in Marigold Yellow, Surf White and Twilight Blue. Actually, you will find Marigold Yellow blending into brown or turquoise, Surf White blending into turquoise, and Twilight Blue with darker blue. In addition, other colors are used as decorative lines or details. All are matte glazed.

A curious decoration has been found on the #3185 vase (see color section). It is on a typical Blended shape and is sprayed, but the colors are Turquoise, Persian Yellow, Marigold Yellow and Rust, reminiscent of Rainbow Ware's use of dinnerware colors, and it is glossy, not matte.

Bowl, oval, 8" x 4"/3175	40–50
Bowl, 12" x 8"/3195	50–60
Candle holder, 4" high, pair/3173	35–50
Candle holder, 4" wide, pair/3196	35–50
Vase, 5" x 10" wide/3185	50–60
Vase, 7"/3171	40–50
Vase, 7"/3189	40–50
Vase, pitcher, 7"/3172	40–50
Vase, pitcher, 10"/3176	50–60
Vase, 7¼"/3190	40–50
Vase, 13"/3153A	70–80
Vase, bud, 4"/3174	20–30

COSMOS (1937) Green Matte, Sand, Satin Blue, Satin Green and Satin White. All pieces in this line are shape #2091 except the ash tray.

Ash tray, 5½"/4033	15–25
Bowl, flat, 12"	35–50
Bowl, low, 6"	15–25
Bowl, low, 7"	20–30
Bowl, low, 14"	40–65
Bowl, miniature, 4"	15-25
Candle holder, 4" diameter, each	15–20
Jardiniere, 5"	15–25
Jardiniere, large, 7"	20–35
Vase, 10"	35–45
Vase, bud, 7"	20–35
Wall Pocket, 8"	35–45

EARLY PENNSYLVANIA TULIP (‹1942) Console sets: either of the 3229 bowls with the 3229 candleholders, and the 3686 bowl with the 3687 candleholders. The tulip was done in one of three colors: blue, pink or yellow.

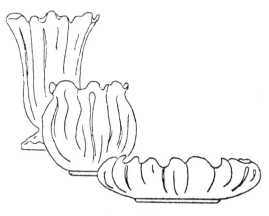

Cosmos/2091

Pricing. Add 10% for blue.

Bowl, Dutch shoe/3258	35
Bowl, octagonal, 11″ x 7″/3695	45
Bowl, oval, 7″/3692	25
Bowl, oval, 9″/3693	30
Bowl, round, 9″/3229–9	25
Bowl, round, 10″/3686	30
Bowl, round, 12½″/3229–12½	35
Candle holder, each/3229	25
Candle holder, each/3687	25
Candy box, round/3684	50
Candy box, square/3676	45
Jar, covered/3689	45
Pig Bank, 4″/1076B	
Carved	125
Not carved	50–75
Pig Cactus/1076C	75–100
Pitcher Vase, 6″/3211	40
Vase, 5″/3691	35
Vase, 5″/3694	35
Vase, 5″/3682	35
Vase, 5½″/3266	40
Vase, 7″/3688	50
Vase, 7″/3683	50

Vase, 7″/3685	50
Vase, 9″/3690	65
Vase, 9″/3696	65
Vase, 11″/3681	75
Vase, Watering Pot, 7¼″/3510	75
Vase, Watering Pot, 10″/3511	125

FLOWER WARE (1935) Blue of the Sky, Colonial Blue, Green Matte, Satin Blue, Rust, Satin White, Silver Green, Surf White, Tangerine and Yellow. Some of these may be found in multicolors a lá the flower ash trays. See also Early Giftware/Cosmos and Tulip, and Smoking Items.

Bowl, Marsh Rose, 14″/1873	15–25
Bowl, Petunia, 12″/1871	35–50
Bowl, Wild Rose, 8″/1874	15–25
Bowl, Zinnia, 10″/1872	20–30
Candle holder, flower, 4″/1875	20–35
Candle holder/Vase, Phlox/1879	20–35
Flower Block/1876	20–30
Candle holder, flower, 4″/1875	20–35
Candle holder/Vase, Phlox/1879	20–35
Flower Block/1876	20–30

MADONNAS (1940) These are combination Madonnas and vases. They seem to have been in production for only a year, which would account for their scarcity. According to the catalog, they were made in Satin White only. One or two hand-decorated Madonnas have been found; prices for these are ND.

Bust, hands clasped, 9″/3204	75
Bust, holding infant, 8¼″/3231	75
Bust, in relief, 8″/3232	50
Figure, hands clasped, 10″/3205	50
Figure, holding infant, 9½″/3206	75
Figure, seated, w/infant, 9¾″/3230	75

Marsh Rose/1873

Petunia Bowl/1871

Wild Rose Bowl/1874

Zenia (Zinnia) Bowl/1872

Flower candle holder/1875

Phlox vase/candle
holder/1879

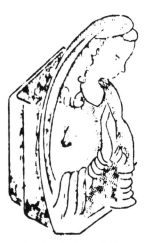

Bust, hands clasped/3204

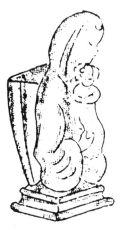

Bust, holding infant/3231

Bust, in relief/3232

Figure, hands clasped/3205

Figure, holding infant/3206

Figure, seated,
w/infant/3230

91

MINIATURES & WHATNOTS (1940) Stangl made many small pieces, but these fifteen were designated Miniatures & Whatnots in the 1940 catalog; some had already appeared in earlier catalogs. Originally available at 25 cents each, they will be found in at least the following colors: Colonial Blue, Silver Green, Tangerine, Persian Yellow and Satin White. Some have also been seen in Antique Gold.

Bowl, Tulip, 2¼″/3208	10–15
Flower pot, w/saucer, 1¾″/1792	10–15
Jug, 1¾″/1902	10–15
Jug, 2″/2000	10–15
Jug, 2¼″/1388	10–15
Jug, 2½″/3235	10–15
Jug, 3″/3053	10–15
Jug, ball, 2½″/3233	10–15
Pig Cactus, 1½″/1745	30–35
Vase, 2″/2011	10–15
Vase, 3″/3054	10–15
Vase, 3″/3055	10–15
Vase, 3″/3234	10–15
Vase, Cornucopia, 2¼″/3209	10–15
Vase, Tulip, 2¾″/3207	10–15

#1388   #1902   #2000   #3233

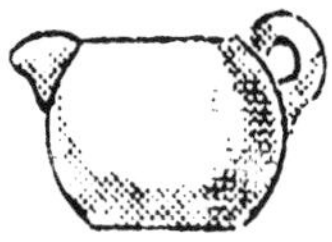

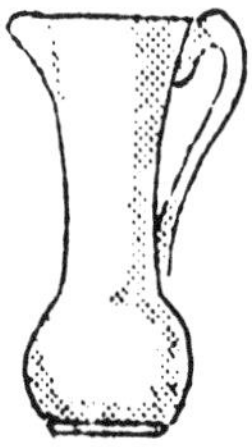

#3053   #3055   #3054   #3234

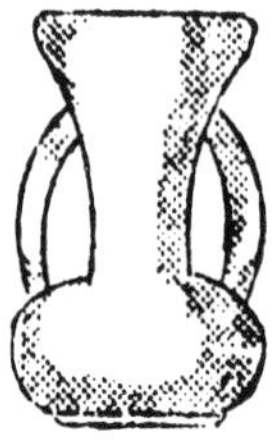

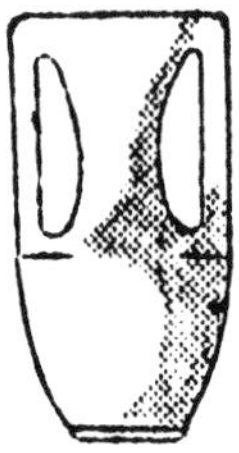

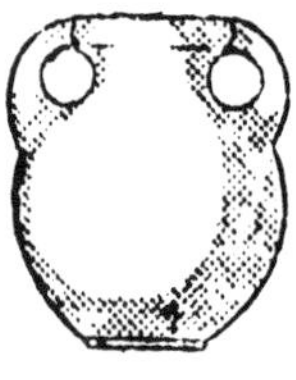

#2011   #1792   #3209   #3207

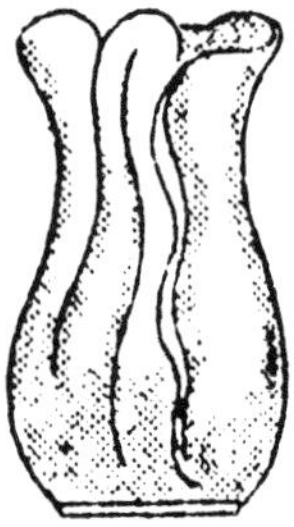

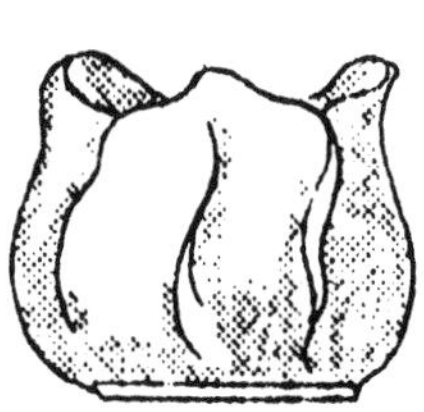

#3208   #3235   #1745

MISCELLANY These are some of the wide variety of items you will find. The #1919 flower pot and #1999 vase have a frog attached to the inside of the pieces. Most of these items will be found in the Shape Library.

Pricing. Candleholders are priced singly.

Ash tray/1658	15–25
Ash tray/1954	8–15
Ash tray/1958	8–15
Ash tray/candy, 8″/3240	15–25
Ash tray, Shell/2022	8–15
Basket, 7″/3225	25–50
Basket, 9″/3226	30–50
Basket, 11″/3251	40–75
Basket, 11″/3253	40–85
Basket, 12″/3252	40–85
Bowl, 5″/3256	10–20
Bowl, 6″/3094	15–25
Bowl, 7½″/3228	15–25
Bowl, 9″/3283	20–35
Bowl, cradle, 7″ x 4″/2060	25–45
Bowl, Dutch shoe/3258	20–35
Bowl, footed, 2″/2010	10–15
Bowl, high heel shoe/3259	25–40
Bowl, oval, zigzag handles/3175	25–45
Bowl, ruffled, 7″/1919	20–40
Bowl, scallop, round, 8″/2050	20–35
Bowl, shell, 6½″ x 2¼″/3255	15–25
Bowl, 3 step feet/1740	45–75
Candle holder, 4″/2059	15–25
Candle holder, cradle/2061	15–25
Candle holder, double, 6½″ high/2054	20–35
Candle holder, oblong/2058	15–25
Candle holder, scallop, round, 2½″/2051	15–25
Candle holder, zigzag handles, 4″/3173	20–30
Flower pot w/saucer, 8″/1642	25–50
Flower pot w/saucer, 8″/1792	25–50
Flower pot, 8″/1515	25–50
Match holder, Dog/3534	300 +
Match holder, Pony/3549	300 +
Match holder, Rabbit/3533	300 +
Pitcher, Rabbit	150
Pitcher, zigzag handle, 7″/3172	15–35
Pitcher, zig zag handle, 10″/3176	35–50

Server, Leaf, 8″/3239	12–20
Vase, 2″/2011	10–15
Vase, 2″/2012	10–15
Vase, 2″/2014	10–15
Vase, 3″/2017	15–25
Vase, 3″/2019	15–25
Vase, 3″/2020	15–25
Vase, 3″/2021	15–25
Vase, 3½″/2016	15–25
Vase, 4″/2018	15–25
Vase, 4″ bud, zigzag handles/3174	15–25
Vase, 4½″ twist, 3 balls/2047	15–25
Vase, 5″ fish on base/3613	35–75
Vase, 5½″/3112	15–25
Vase, 5½″/3266	15–25
Vase, 6″ pitcher/3211	15–25
Vase, 6″ scroll horn/2056	15–25
Vase, 6½″/3110	20–35
Vase, 6½″/3111	20–35
Vase, 6½″/3139	15–30
Vase, 7″/3104	20–35
Vase, 7″/3189	25–45
Vase, 7″/3215	15–25
Vase, 7″/3217	20–35
Vase, 7″/3218	20–35
Vase, 7″/3219	20–35
Vase, 7″/3220	20–35
Vase, 7″ Acanthus/1540	20–35
Vase, 7″ ruffled/1999	25–45
Vase, 7″ 3 twist handles/1124	50–100
Vase, 7″ zigzag handles/3171	20–35
Vase, 7¼″/3103	20–35
Vase, 7¼″ round watering can/3510	25–60
Vase, 8″/3214	12–25
Vase, 8″/3216	15–30
Vase, 8″/3612	15–30
Vase, 8″/3441	25–40
Vase, 8″ scroll handles, square base/2041	20–40
Vase, 10″ tall watering can/3511	50–100
Vase, 11″ duck handles/3148	100–125
Vase, 11″ squirrel handles/3146	100–125
Vase, 12″ urn/1758	65–125
Vase, 13″ zigzag handles/3153	40–60
Vase, 18″ floor, narrow/1329	100–200
Vase, 18″ floor, wide/1329A	100–200
Vase, ball, large/1908	35–65
Vase, oblong flower jar, 10″ x 4″/2057	30–60

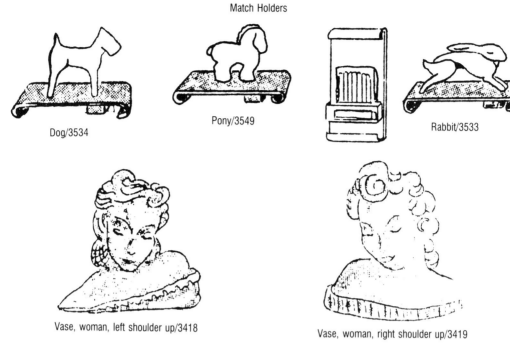

Match Holders

Dog/3534

Pony/3549

Rabbit/3533

Vase, woman, left shoulder up/3418

Vase, woman, right shoulder up/3419

Vase, woman, left shoulder up,
    6"/3418
    Satin White/Glossy White   50
    With green or blue trim   ND
Vase, woman, right shoulder up,
    6"/3419
    Satin White/glossy White   50
    With green or blue trim   ND
Wall pocket, 7"/3236   35–60

RAINBOW WARE (1939) Pieces are glazed in a combination of the basic dinnerware colors of Tangerine Red, Persian Yellow, Silver Green and Colonial Blue. However, the yellow was not often used. On such pieces, the red and green combine to give a brown color.

Pricing. Add 25% for pieces with yellow in them.

Bowl, square base, 2¾"/1392   75
Bowl, ruffled, 6"   100
Bowl, stacked rib, 10½"   100
Bowl, hexagonal, lug handle, 3¼"   75
Candlestick, birds, each/1389   150

Bird candlestick/1389

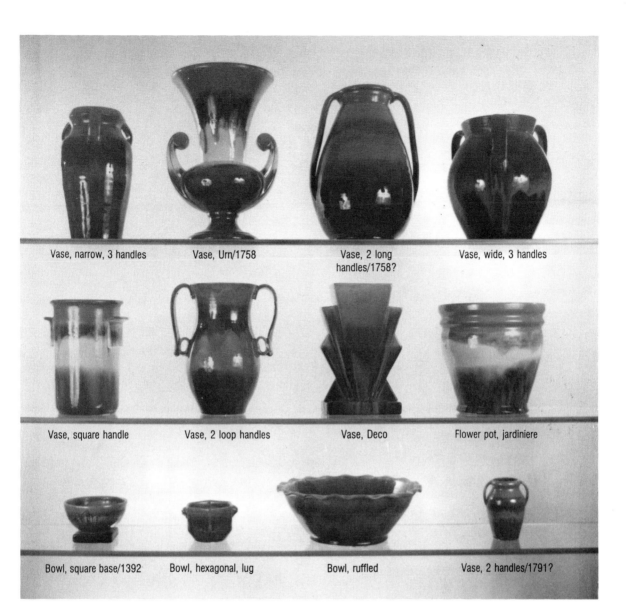

Vase, narrow, 3 handles   Vase, Urn/1758   Vase, 2 long handles/1758?   Vase, wide, 3 handles

Vase, square handle   Vase, 2 loop handles   Vase, Deco   Flower pot, jardiniere

Bowl, square base/1392   Bowl, hexagonal, lug   Bowl, ruffled   Vase, 2 handles/1791?

Dish, horse handle	200
Flower frog, round, 2¾″	50
Flower pot, attached saucer, 7¾″	125
Flower pot, jardiniere style	100
Jar, w/lid, square, 4 feet	150
Planter, camel	500+
Planter, fish, 9″	200
Planter, hanging, 7″	100
Planter, pig, 5¼″	200
Vase, Acanthus, 7″/1540	100
Vase, Acanthus, bud, 6¼″	100
Vase, Deco, 6¼″	125

Vase, Deco, 9¼″	175
Vase, floor, 18″/1329	300
Vase, scallop rim, 4″	75
Vase, square handle, 8″	125
Vase, 2 handles, 4¼″/1791?	75
Vase, 2 handle, low, squat, 5″	125
Vase, 2 high handles, 7½″	175
Vase, 2 long handles, 11″/1758?	150
Vase, 2 loop handles, 9¼″	175
Vase, 3 twist handles, 7″/1124	125
Vase, 3 handles, narrow, 9½″	125
Vase, 3 handles, wide, 9″	150
Vase, Urn, 12″/1758	175

Vase, Acanthus/1540   Bowl, stacked rib   Flower pot, w/saucer

Vase, 3 twist
handles/1124   Planter, hanging   Vase, 2 high handles

Vase, scallop rim   Vase, 2 handle, low,   Dish, horse handle
                       squat

RHYTHMIC LINE (1937) Colors per catalog: Green Matte, Satin Blue, Satin Brown, Satin Green and Satin White. This entire line is shape #2092.

Basket	35–50
Bowl, low, 7″ x 4½″	15–25
Candle holder, pair, 3¼″ high	30–40
Jar, small, 6″	15–25
Jar, large, 9″	25–35
Vase, miniature, 3¼″ high	12–20
Vase, tall, 7″	15–25
Vase, tall, 11″	25–35
Wall Pocket, 6″ x 9″	25–35

SCROLL LINE (1937) Colors per catalog are: Bronze Green, Dusty Pink, Satin Green, Satin White, Tangerine and Yellow.

Bowl, 4-sided, 10″/3047	50–60
Bowl, oval, 6″/3044	25–35
Bowl, oval, 10″/3042	30–40
Bowl, round, 8″/3045	30–40
Candle holder, pair, 3¾″/3046	25–30
Candle holder, double, 10″/3043	50–60

SCROLL LEAF LINE (1937) Catalog lists colors of Rust, Satin Blue, Satin Brown, Satin Green and Satin White.

Bowl, small, rd, 2″ x 2½″/3026	12–20
Bowl, medium, rd, 4″ x 4″/3021	15–25

Bowl, large, rd, 7½″ x 7″/3020	20–30
Bowl, low, 6″/3028	20–30
Bowl, low, 9″/3029	30–40
Candle holder, 2″ x 2½″/3027, each	15–25
Candle holder, 5½″ x 3″/3025, each	20–30
Insert/3031	20–30
Vase, bud, 5½″ x 3″/3024	15–25
Vase, small, 8″ x 3½″/3023	25–35
Vase, medium, 9″ x 4½″/3022	30–40
Vase, tall, 17″/3030	60–75

SPIRAL LINE (1937) Colors per catalog: Bronze Green, Dusty Pink, Satin Green, Satin White, Tangerine and Yellow.

Ash tray, 5″/3041	15–20
Bowl, small, 2½″ x 3″/3038	10–15
Bowl, medium, 3″ x 6″/3037	15–20
Bowl, large, 6½″ x 8″/3035	20–25
Bowl, low, 4″ x 9″/3036	25–30
Bowl, oval, no handles, 7″ x 4½″/3048	20–25
Bowl w/high handles, 6″ x 4½″/3056	40–50
Candle holder, pair, 2½″ x 3″/3039	20–30
Insert/3040	10–15
Vase, medium, 7″/3034	20–30
Vase, tall, 9½″/3033	30–35
Wall Pocket, 7″/3032	ND

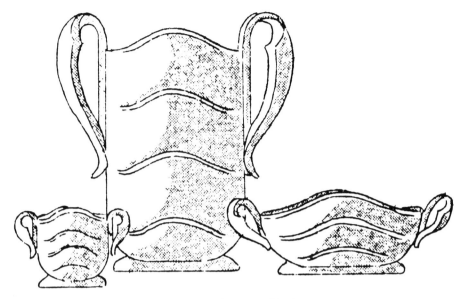

Rhythmic candle holder, vase and bowl

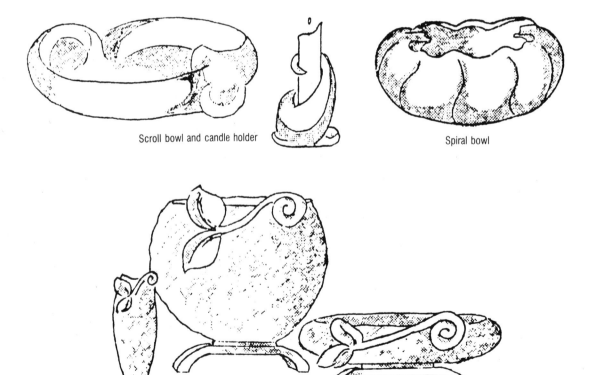

Scroll bowl and candle holder   Spiral bowl

Scroll Leaf bud vase, large round bowl and low bowl

TERRA ROSE (1941) Many pieces in this line were designed by Auguste Jacob. Produced in three colors: Blue, Green and Mauve. A fourth color, Amethyst, was used for the American Way promotion. Terra Rose is decorated in a technique called *glaze on glaze*. First, the piece is cast and fired to the bisque stage; then the color is brushed on. The color might be applied to the outside only, the inside only, or selected portions of the body. Next, an opaque glaze is brushed over the entire body and the piece is fired a second time. By brushing rather than spraying this glaze, the red bisque shows milky pink and the colored portions come through. The milky effect in the glaze is achieved by zirconia which is an opacifier.

Generally, only one Terra Rose color was used on a piece, but pieces with two colors (such as match holders) will be found.

The #3520 and #3521 ash trays can be used as lids for the #3520 cigarette box. Terra Rose dinnerware was made on the coupe and Piecrust shapes. Many of these items will be found in the Shape Library. See also Birds and Special Orders/Lunning.

Ash tray, Flower, 5½″ x 5″/3526	20
Ash tray, Leaf, 3¼″ x 3″/3528	15
Ash tray, Leaf, 3½″ square/3531	15
Ash tray, Leaf, 4″ x 3½″/3529	15
Ash tray, Leaf, 4¼″ x 3″/3527	15
Ash tray, Leaf, 4½″ x 4″/3520	15
Ash tray, Leaf, 5¼″ x 4¼″/3524	20
Ash tray, Leaf, 5½″ x 4″/3525	20
Ash tray, Leaf, 5½″ x 4″/3521	20
Ash tray, Leaf, 5¾″ x 4½″/3532	20
Ash tray, Leaf, 6¼″ x 4″/3523	20
Ash tray, Oak leaf, 4″ x 2¾″/3530	15
Ash tray, Shell/2022	15
Ash tray, Shell, 5″ x 4½″/3522	15
Basket, 8″/3495	40
Basket, 11″ x 9″/3251	75
Basket, 12½″ x 7½″/3414	55
Basket, Leaf, 14″ x 7½″/3427	85
Bowl, 7½″/3228	20
Bowl, 8″/3495A	25
Bowl, 10″ x 7½″/3426	35
Bowl, 11½″/3706	50
Bowl, 12″ x 5″/3439	50

Bowl, 12½″/3414A	35
Bowl, Leaf, 11½″ x 8″/3496	45
Bowl, Leaf, 12″ x 9″/3539	45
Bowl, Leaf, 12¾″ x 7½″/3541	40
Bowl, Leaf, 12″ x 9½″/3542	45
Bowl, Leaf, 13″ x 7¾″/3540	45
Bowl, Leaf, 16″ x 10″/3429	50
Bowl, Leaf, 16″ x 13″/3535	60
Bowl, Leaf, 18″ x 11″/3537	60
Bowl, Leaf, 18″ x 12½″/3536	60
Bowl, Oak Leaf, 17″ x 13″/3538	60
Bowl, octagonal, 11″ x 7″/3695	35
Bowl, Shell, 9″ x 5½″/3498	35
Bowl, Shell, 10″ x 5″/3512	35
Bowl, Shell, 12½″ x 5″/3438	45
Candle holder, 3½″/3428	35
Candle holder, pr, 4″/3497	30
Candle holder, pr, 4½″/3499	30
Candle holder, Rhythmic, pr, 3¼″/2092	40
Candlestick, Tulip, tall	35
Cigarette Box, 4″ x 3½″/3520	35
Dish, Apple, single, 6½″/3552	15
Dish, Apple, double, 12″/3550	25
Dish, Pear, single, 7¾″/3553	20
Dish, Pear, double, 11″/3551	30
Match holder, Dog/3534	300+
Match holder, Pony/3549	300+
Match holder, Rabbit/3533	300+
Server, Clam Shell, 10½″/3789	35
Server, Snail Shell, 13¾″/3736	60
Vase, 2¾″ Shell/3255	20
Vase, 5¼″/3613	45
Vase, 5½″/3514	30
Vase, 6″/3442	20
Vase, 6″ Cornucopia/2056	20
Vase, 6″ Fleur-de-Lis/3417	20
Vase, 6½″/3139	30
Vase, 6½″/3411	25
Vase, 6¾″/3503	35
Vase, 7″/3563	20
Vase, 7″ Cosmos/3413	25
Vase, 7¼″ round watering can/3510	45
Vase, 7½″/3515	30
Vase, 7½″/3565	22
Vase, 8″/3441	25
Vase, 8″/3612	20
Vase, 8½″ Shell/3614	50
Vase, 8¾″/3436	40
Vase, 8¾″ Fleur-de-Lis/3416	30

Mountain Goat Head vase

Horse Head vase

Vase, 9″/3415	40	Vase, 11″/3422	45
Vase, 9½″/3437	35	Vase, 11″/3502	45
Vase, 9½″/3675	55	Vase, 12″/3440	50
Vase, 10″/3421	40	Vase, 13″ Horse Head/3611	350
Vase, 10″/3566	50	Vase, 14¾″ Mountain Goat Head/3708	350
Vase, 10½″/3615	55	Warmer, square/3412	10

TROPICAL WARE (‹1935) Produced for a very short time, perhaps only a year. Available in two-color combinations of Blue and Yellow, Dark Green and Eggplant, Blue and Tangerine, and Oyster White and Eggplant.

Bowl, cut-out foot/1945	85
Bowl, footed, 8″/2028	100

Bowl, 3 feet, 7″/2023	85
Candle holder, pair/1945	45
Vase, 7″/2024	100
Vase, 8″/2026	100
Vase, 8″/2027	100
Vase, Criss Cross, 7″/1944–7	100
Vase, Criss Cross, 9″/1944–9	125
Vase, Cylinder, 8″/2025	100
Vase, 4 handles, 7″/1942	100

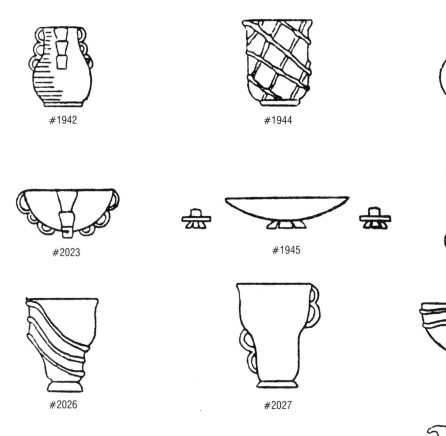

#1942

#1944

#2024

#2023

#1945

#2025

#2026

#2027

#2028

TULIP LINE Colonial Blue, Rust, Satin Blue, Satin White, Silver Green, Surf White, Tangerine and Persian Yellow. See also Miniatures.

Bowl, small, 4″ high/1878	15–25
Bowl, medium, 5½″ high/1878	20–30
Bowl, large, 7″ high/1878	25–35
Vase, tall, 12″/2049	40–50

Tulip bowl and vase.

Late Giftware

Items in this section were introduced in the fifties and sixties.

APPLIQUÉ (ca 1964) Intended to resemble Wedgwood. Made in two solid colors: Blue (either gloss or semi-matte) or Jade Green.

Cigarette box/3898	45
Cigarette holder/3996	20
Cigarette lighter/5153	35
Jug, 5″/4060	25
Jug, 7″/5152–7	35
Jug, 8″/4056	40
Jug, 9″/5152–9	45
Tray, round, 7″/5058	25
Tray, round, 7″/5154	25
Tray, oval/3997	20
Tray, square, 4½″/3666	20
Vase, 7″/4007	30
Vase, bud, 8″/4050	35

CARIBBEAN Light blue and light green sponged finish.

Ash tray, 6″ x 4″/1954	8
Ash tray, 12½″ x 6½″/5004	16
Ash tray, oblong, 4¼″/1953	8
Ash tray, oval, 8½″/3942	12
Ash tray, square, 4½″/5173	8
Ash tray, square, 7″/5174	10
Ash tray, square, 9″/3915	16
Bowl, 10¼″/4062	20
Bowl, Cosmos, 12″/5139	25
Bowl, flower shape, 7″/3410–7	20
Bowl, flower shape, 9″/3410–9	25
Bowl, scallop, 9″/2064	16
Bowl, Tulip, 4″/5144	12
Candle holder, pair, 2″/5069	28
Candle holder, pair, 2½″/5138	30
Dish, apple, single/3785	12
Dish, apple, double/3784	16
Dish, Clover, 3-part/3857	12
Dish, pear, single/3783	12
Dish, pear, double/3782	16
Dish, square, w/lid/3676	28
Grecian urn, 8″/2041	16
Horn of Plenty, 7¼″/5065	20
Pitcher, 8¼″/4056	16

Pitcher, 11¾″/4055	20
Pitcher, 12″/4053	24
Server, center handle, 10″/5151	8
Server, Leaf, 8″ x 7″/3859	12
Server, two tier/5156	16
Shell, 5½″/4037	10
Shell, 7½″/4018	12
Tray, Ivy Leaf, 3-part/5146	12
Vase, 9¾″ Phoenician/5023	20
Vase, bud, 8″/4050	16
Vase, bud, 9¾″/5093	20
Vase, chalice, 6¼″/5190	16
Vase, Cosmos, 7½″/5134	20

GOLD AND SILVER (ca 1957–1977) Kay Hackett: "That Antique Gold, Stangl wanted me to use gold on earthenware. And I did a lot of experimenting and finally came up with this dry brush technique, finding that when I put it over a bit of curving, you got a big effect. And it was very simple to do this, of course everybody had to be taught just how to do it." Granada Gold and Black Gold were developed by James Paul, general manager, after the successful introduction of Antique Gold.

I have used Stangl's descriptions; note that "footed" most often means a stem-like foot.

Pricing. Candleholders and candlesticks are priced per pair.

Antique/Granada Gold. Antique Gold is over a satin green glaze and Granada Gold is over a satin tan glaze. The gold used was 22 carat. Every item listed here was made in both finishes, except the 14½″ chop plates, which were made in Antique Gold only. The black in the deep areas of these plates is achieved by extra heavy application of the gold.

Pricing. The cigarette sets are priced for one holder and two ash trays. The Basket Weave, Lion and Stag are shaped like chests. Almost everything made in Antique Gold was also made in Granada Gold; subtract 10% for Granada Gold prices.

Ash tray, Cosmos, 5½″/4033	10
Ash tray, double well, 8¾″ x 4″/5076	15
Ash tray, fluted, 5″/3898–5	10
Ash tray, fluted, 7″/3898–7	15

Butterflies

Ash tray, Leaf, 5½″/4032	10
Ash tray, Leaf, 5½″/4035	10
Ash tray, Leaf, 6″/4036	10
Ash tray, Leaf, 6½″/4034	10
Ash tray, oblong, 4¼″/1953	10
Ash tray, oblong, 6″/1954	10
Ash tray, oblong, 6½″ x 4½″/5097	10
Ash tray, oblong, 7½″ x 5″/5044	10
Ash tray, oblong, 8½″ x 5¼″/5077	15
Ash tray, oblong, 12½″ x 6½″/5004	20
Ash tray, oval, 6″/5116S	8

Clipper Ship

Ash tray, oval, 7″/5116M	10
Ash tray, oval, 8″/5116L	15
Ash tray, oval, 8½″/3942	15
Ash tray, oval, 10½″/3926	20
Ash tray, oval, 11¼″/3976	20
Ash tray, pipe and cigar, 7″ x 9″/5172	25
Ash tray, prism, 6″ x 4″/5075	12
Ash tray, round, 4⅝″/5056	12
Ash tray, round, 5⅜″/5057	12
Ash tray, round, 7¼″/5058	15
Ash tray, round, 8¼″/5060	15
Ash tray, round, 8½″/3973	15
Ash tray, round, 9¼″/5002	20
Ash tray, round, 10″/3972	20
Ash tray, round, 11¼″/4026	20
Ash tray, round, 12½″/4027	22
Ash tray, safety, 6″/3977S	8
Ash tray, safety, 7¼″/3977M	10
Ash tray, safety, 8½″/3977L	15
Ash tray, Scotty/2089	50
Ash tray, shell, 5½″/4037	10
Ash tray, square, 4½″/5173	10
Ash tray, square, 5″/3897–4	10
Ash tray, square, 6″/5074	10
Ash tray, square, 6¼″/5043	10
Ash tray, square, 6½″/3897–6	12
Ash tray, square, 7″/5174	12
Ash tray, square, 7½″/5005	10
Ash tray, square, 9″/3914	20
Ash tray, square, 9″/3915	20
Ash tray, triangle, 5½″/3906	15
Ash tray, triangle, 6½″/3938S	8
Ash tray, triangle, 6¾″/5259	15
Ash tray, triangle, 7″/3904S	8
Ash tray, triangle, 7½″/3938M	10
Ash tray, triangle, 7½″/5017	10
Ash tray, triangle, 8″/3938L	15
Ash tray, triangle, 8″/3904M	10
Ash tray, triangle, 9¼″/3904L	15
Ash tray, windproof, 5¾″/5260	15
Basket, 5½″/3621	35
Basket (Rhythm), 10¼″/3413	45
Bowl, 6″/3229–6	20
Bowl, 6¾″/5040	25
Bowl, 7″/5061	20
Bowl, 8″/4061	25
Bowl, 8″/5039	30
Bowl, 8¼″/3980	20
Bowl, 9″/3229–9	25

Bowl, 9″/3983	25
Bowl, 9½″/5062	30
Bowl, 10¼″/4062	25
Bowl, 11¼″/4065	35
Bowl, 12″/3229-12	35
Bowl, conch shell, 10″/5214	35
Bowl, Cosmos, 12″/5139	30
Bowl, elongated, 13″/5137	35
Bowl, flower shape, 7″/3410–7	25
Bowl, flower shape, 9″ /3410–9	30
Bowl, footed, 5¼″/5029	20
Bowl, footed, 6″/5038	25
Bowl, footed, 6¼″/5030	25
Bowl, footed, 8¼″/5031	35
Bowl, footed, 9″/4028	35
Bowl, footed, 10″/4029	35
Bowl, footed, 10½″/5041	45
Bowl, footed, oval, 6″/5045	15
Bowl, footed, ruffled, 8″/4096	30
Bowl, footed, ruffled, 10″/4095	40
Bowl, fruit, handled/5105	40
Bowl, oval, 8″/5036	15
Bowl, oval, 11¼″/5115	25
Bowl, oval, 14″/5115	35
Bowl, oval, 17½″/5115	45
Bowl, ruffled, 10″/4084	40
Bowl, scallop, oblong, 9″/2064	20
Bowl, scallop, round, 7″/3283	15
Bowl, scallop, round, 8″/2050	25
Bowl, scallop, round, 9″/3283	20
Bowl, Tulip, 5½″/5145	20
Bowl, Tulip, 4″/5144	15
Bowl w/lid/5105	90
Bowl, Zinnia, 10″/1872	35
Candle holder, finger ring, w/glass globe /5287	25
Candle holder, 2″/5069	35
Candle holder, Cosmos, pr, 2½″/5138	35
Candle holder, 3″/5070	35
Candle holder, footed shell, 3″/5212	35
Candle holder, 3½″ (1388)/5194	35
Candle holder, 4″/4064	30
Candle holder, ruffled, footed, 3⅞″/4083	35
Candlestick, 7½″/4016	40
Candlestick, 7½″/5299	40
Cigarette box, 4″ x 5″/3630	25
Cigarette box, fluted	25
Cigarette lighter, 4″/5153	25
Cigarette set, Basket Weave/4088	35

Grape

Cigarette set, Lion/4085	45
Cigarette set, Stag/4089	45
Cigarette set, urn holder/3992	25
Coaster/Ash tray, 5″/4070	10
Compote, 6½″ (1388)/4021	20
Compote, 7″/5063	25
Compote, 8½″ footed shell/5211	35
Compote, 9½″/5064	35
Dish, apple, single/3785	15
Dish, apple, double/3784	20
Dish, candy, footed, ruffled, 5″/4075	15
Dish, candy, footed, ruffled, 7″/4076	20

Strawberry

Dish, candy, ruffled, 7″/4077	15	Server, Leaf, 12″/4039	25
Dish, candy, ruffled, 8″4078	20	Server, Leaf, 13½″/4038	30
Dish, candy w/fruit lid/5180	35	Server, Leaf, 14½″/3779	35
Dish, candy w/lid/3676	35	Server, Leaf, 16″/4042	40
Dish, candy w/lid/5188	30	Server, Leaf, 17″/4041	45
Dish, candy w/lid, 6½″/4092	35	Server, two tier/5156	20
Dish, candy w/lid, 8″/4091	35	Shell, 5½″/4037	12
Dish, candy w/lid, 11″/4069	45	Shell, 7½″/4018	15
Dish, footed shell, 3″/5213	25	Shell, 9⅛″/4019	20
Dish, heart, 8″/3788	20	Shell, 10½″/4020	25
Dish, pear, single/3783	15	Tray, apple, 13″/3546	30
Dish, pear, double/3782	20	Tray, double leaf, 9½″/1800–D	22
Dish, scallop, 5″/5162	15	Tray, triple leaf, 12″/1800–T	30
Dish, scallop, 7″/5163	20	Tray, fruit, 15″/3774	25
Dish, snack/3786	15	Tray, Ivy Leaf, 3-part/5146	15
Dish, snack, heart shape/3787	12	Tumbler/5160	15
Dish, triple shell/3781	35	Urn, 3″/2048	10
Flower pot, 4″/4071–4	10	Urn, 10″/5042	30
Flower pot, 5″ /4071–5	15	Vase, 3″/2019	10
Flower pot, 7″ /4071–7	20	Vase, 3½″/2016	10
Ginger jar, 5½″/5015	25	Vase, 4″ Tulip/5144	15
Ginger jar, 7¼″/5016	35	Vase, 4½″/3689	15
Grecian urn, 8″/2041	20	Vase, 5″ ball/1907	12
Horn of Plenty, 7¼″/5065	25	Vase, 5″/3691	15
Horn of Plenty, 10″/5066	40	Vase, 5″/3694	15
Horn of Plenty, 10½″/3617	35	Vase, 5⅛″/4004	15
Lightswitch plate, single/5195	10	Vase, 5½″/3112	12
Lightswitch plate, double/5196	15	Vase, 5½″/3113	12
Pencil cup, 4″/3952	8	Vase, 5½″/3117	12
Pitcher, 5¼″/4060	20	Vase, 5½″/3222	10
Pitcher, 6¼″/4059	25	Vase, 5½″ petal/3224	15
Pitcher, 7½″/4058	20	Vase, 5¾″ ruffled/4080	20
Pitcher, 8¼″/4056	20	Vase, 5¾″ bud/5012	10
Pitcher, 11¼″/4055	25	Vase, 5¾″ bud/5093	10
Pitcher, 12″/4053	35	Vase, 5¾″ ruffled/4079	25
Pitcher, 14½″/4052	35	Vase, 6″ urn/3987	15
Pitcher, 16″/4054	40	Vase, 6¼″/4002	15
Planter, French phone, 8½″/5303	60	Vase, 6¼″ chalice/5190	20
Planter, Swan, 3½″/5035	15	Vase, 6½″ Fleur-de-Lis/3417	12
Planter, Swan, 5″/5034	20	Vase, 6¾″ bud/3981	15
Planter, Swan, 6¾″/5033	25	Vase, 6¾″/4007	20
Planter, Swan, 9¾″/5032	35	Vase, 6⅞″ footed/5021	15
Plate, Butterflies, 14½″/5028	100	Vase, 7″ scallop/2067	15
Plate, Clipper Ship, 14½″/5027	100	Vase, 7″/3685	35
Plate, Grape, 14½″/5026	75	Vase, 7″/3984	20
Plate, Strawberry, 14½″/5025	75	Vase, 7¼″ urn/1906	15
Server, center handle, 10″/5151	10	Vase, 7¼″ flared/3218	20
Server, Clover, 7″/3857	20	Vase, 7¼″/3989	20
Server, Leaf, 8″/3859	15	Vase, 7¼″ bud/5013	20

Vase, 7½″ bud/1905	12
Vase, 7½″ handled/3103	25
Vase, 7½″ flared/3217	20
Vase, 7½″ oval/3220	22
Vase, 7½″ milk can/canister/3688	25
Vase, 7½″ urn/4025	20
Vase, 7½″ bud/5094	10
Vase, 7½″ spiral base/5133	20
Vase, 7½″ Cosmos/5134	20
Vase, 7½″ flared/5135	15
Vase, 7½″ Scroll Horn/5136	15
Vase, 7¾″/5022	15
Vase, 8″ bud/4050	20
Vase, 8¼″ ruffled, footed/4081	35
Vase, 8½″ swirl/1574	30
Vase, 8¾″ bud/4051	25
Vase, 8¾″ bud/5014	25
Vase, 9″ oval/3264	25
Vase, 9″ ribbed/3265	25
Vase, 9″ Fleur-de-Lis/3416	20
Vase, 9″/3979	30
Vase, 9″/5104	25
Vase, 9¼″ bud/4049	20
Vase, 9¼″/5024	25
Vase, 9¼″/5037	40
Vase, 9½″ cloverleaf/2052	20
Vase, 9¾″ Phoenician/5023	25
Vase, 10″/5036	35
Vase, 10½″ flared/5132	25
Vase, 12″/3993	45
Vase, 13″ Horse head/3611	250
Vase, double shell/3672	45
Wall fount, Boy w/Dolphin, 15″/5169H	65
Wall bowl for above, 8¼″ wide/5169B	30
Wall fount, Ram's Head,	
12¾″ x 11½″/5170H	125
Wall bowl for above, 13″ wide/5170B	40

Standard shape used for commemorative ash tray made for Geigy's 200th anniversary.

Ash tray, oblong, 8½″ x 5¼″/5077	15
Ash tray, oblong, 12½″ x 6½″/5004	20
Ash tray, oval, 6″/5116S	8
Ash tray, oval, 7″/5116M	10
Ash tray, oval, 8″/5116L	15
Ash tray, oval, 8½″/3942	15
Ash tray, prism, 6″ x 4″/5075	12
Ash tray, round, 7¼″/5058	15
Ash tray, round, 8¼″/5060	15
Ash tray, round, 10″/3972	20
Ash tray, round, 11¼″/4026	20
Ash tray, shell, 5½″/4037	10
Ash tray, square, 4½″/5173	10
Ash tray, square, 5″/3897–4	10
Ash tray, square, 6″/5074	10

Black Gold   Black Gold is 22-carat gold over a black glaze. The earliest listing I have found for Black Gold is 1968; it was not in a 1965 catalog.

Ash tray, Cosmos, 5½″/4033	10
Ash tray, double well, 8¾″ x 4″/5076	15
Ash tray, fluted, 5″/3898–5	10
Ash tray, Leaf, 6½″/4034	10
Ash tray, oblong, 4¼″/1953	10
Ash tray, oblong, 6″/1954	10
Ash tray, oblong, 6½″ x 4½″/5097	10

Ash tray, square, 6½″/3897–6	12	Planter, Swan, 3½″/5035	15
Ash tray, square, 7″/5174	12	Planter, Swan, 5″/5034	20
Ash tray, square, 9″/3915	20	Server, center handle, 10″/5151	10
Ash tray, triangle, 6¾″/5259	15	Server, Clover, 7″/3857	20
Ash tray, windproof, 5¾″/5260	15	Server, Leaf, 8″/3859	15
Basket, 5½″/3621	35	Server, Leaf, 12″/4039	25
Bowl, 8″/4061	25	Server, Leaf, 13½″/4038	30
Bowl, 8¼″/3980	20	Server, Leaf, 16″/4042	40
Bowl, 10¼″/4062	25	Server, Leaf, 17″/4041	45
Bowl, conch shell, 10″/5214	35	Server, two tier/5156	20
Bowl, Cosmos, 12″/5139	30	Shell, 5½″/4037	12
Bowl, flower shape, 7″/3410–7	25	Shell, 7½″/4018	15
Bowl, flower shape, 9″/3410–9	30	Tray, apple, 13″/3546	30
Bowl, oval, 11¼″/5115S	25	Tray, double leaf, 9½″/1800–D	22
Bowl, oval, 14″/5115–M	35	Tray, triple leaf, 12″/1800–T	30
Bowl, scallop, oblong, 9″/2064	20	Tray, Ivy Leaf, 3-part/5146	15
Bowl, Tulip, 5½″/5145	20	Urn, 3″/2048	10
Bowl, Tulip, 4″/5144	15	Vase, 3″/2019	10
Bowl, Zinnia, 10″/1872	35	Vase, 3½″/2016	10
Candle holder, 2″/5069	35	Vase, 4″ Tulip/5144	15
Candle holder, Cosmos, pr, 2½″/5138	35	Vase, 4½″/3689	15
Candle holder, footed shell, 3″/5212	35	Vase, 5″ ball/1907	12
Candle holder, 3½″ (1388)/5194	35	Vase, 5″/3691	15
Cigarette box, 4″ x 5″/3630	25	Vase, 5″/3694	15
Cigarette lighter, 4″/5153	25	Vase, 5½″/3112	12
Compote, 6½″ (1388)/4021	20	Vase, 5½″/3113	12
Compote, 8½″ footed shell/5211	35	Vase, 5½″/3117	12
Dish, apple, single/3785	15	Vase, 5½″ petal/3224	15
Dish, apple, double/3784	20	Vase, 5¾″ bud/5093	10
Dish, candy w/fruit lid/5180	35	Vase, 6″ urn/3987	15
Dish, candy w/lid/3676	35	Vase, 6¼″ chalice/5190	20
Dish, candy w/lid/5188	30	Vase, 7″ scallop/2067	15
Dish, candy w/lid, 6½″/4092	35	Vase, 7″/3685	35
Dish, footed shell, 3″/5213	25	Vase, 7¼″ urn/1906	15
Dish, pear, single/3783	15	Vase, 7¼″ flared/3218	20
Dish, pear, double/3782	20	Vase, 7½″ bud/1905	12
Dish, snack, heart shape/3787	12	Vase, 7½″ handled/3103	25
Grecian urn, 8″/2041	20	Vase, 7½″ flared/3217	20
Horn of Plenty, 7¼″/5065	25	Vase, 7½″ oval/3220	22
Horn of Plenty, 10″/5066	40	Vase, 7½″ milk can/canister/3688	25
Lightswitch plate, single/5195	10	Vase, 7½″ Cosmos/5134	20
Lightswitch plate, double/5196	15	Vase, 7½″ flared/5135	15
Pitcher, 5¼″/4060	20	Vase, 8″ bud/4050	20
Pitcher, 6¼″/4059	25	Vase, 8½″ swirl/1574	30
Pitcher, 8¼″/4056	20	Vase, 9″ oval/3264	25
Pitcher, 11¼″/4055	25	Vase, 9″ ribbed/3265	25
Pitcher, 12″/4053	35	Vase, 9¾″ Phoenician/5023	25
Pitcher, 16″/4054	40	Vase, double shell/3672	45

Colonial Silver (Platina). Some time after its introduction, Platina was changed to Colonial Silver (silver dry-brushed over a gray body) because silver was cheaper than platinum. As platinum resembles silver, there is no way to tell the difference, except for the mark.

Ash tray, Cosmos, 5½"/4033	8
Ash tray, oblong, 4¼"/1953	8
Ash tray, oblong, 6"/1954	8
Ash tray, oblong, 6½" x 4½"/5097	8
Ash tray, oblong, 12½" x 6½"/5004	16
Ash tray, oval, 8½"/3942	12
Ash tray, prism, 6" x 4"/5075	10
Ash tray, round, 8¼"/5060	12
Ash tray, round, 10"/3972	16
Ash tray, round, 11¼"/4026	16
Ash tray, shell, 5½"/4037	8
Ash tray, square, 7"/5174	10
Ash tray, square, 9"/3915	16
Ash tray, triangle, 6¾"/5259	12
Ash tray, windproof, 5¾"/5260	12
Basket, 5½"/3621	30
Basket (Rhythm), 10¼"/3413	35
Bowl, Cosmos, 12"/5139	25
Bowl, flower shape, 7"/3410–7	22
Bowl, flower shape, 9"/3410–9	28
Bowl, oval, 11¼"/5115S	22
Bowl, oval, 14"/5115M	30
Bowl, scallop, oblong, 9"/2064	16
Bowl, Tulip, 5½"/5145	16
Bowl, Tulip, 4"/5144	12
Candle holder, 2"/5069	30
Candle holder, Cosmos, pr, 2½"/5138	30
Candle holder, 3½" (1388)/5194	30
Cigarette box, 4" x 5"/3630	22
Cigarette lighter, 4"/5153	22
Dish, apple, single/3785	12
Dish, apple, double/3784	16
Dish, candy w/fruit lid/5180	30
Dish, candy w/lid/3676	30
Dish, candy w/lid/5188	28
Dish, footed shell, 3"/5213	25
Dish, pear, single/3783	12
Dish, pear, double/3782	16
Grecian urn, 8"/2041	18
Horn of Plenty, 7¼"/5065	22
Horn of Plenty, 10"/5066	35
Pitcher, 5¼"/4060	12

Pitcher, 6¼"/4059	14
Pitcher, 8¼"/4056	16
Pitcher, 11¼"/4055	22
Planter, Swan, 5"/5034	20
Server, center handle, 10"/5151	8
Server, Clover, 7"/3857	16
Server, Leaf, 8"/3859	12
Server, Leaf, 13½"/4038	25
Server, two tier/5156	15
Shell, 5½"/4037	10
Shell, 7½"/4018	12
Tray, double leaf, 9½"/1800–D	18
Tray, triple leaf, 12"/1800–T	20
Tray, Ivy Leaf, 3-part/5146	12
Vase, 4" Tulip/5144	12
Vase, 5¾" bud/5093	8
Vase, 6¼" chalice/5190	16
Vase, 7¼" urn/1906	12
Vase, 7¼" flared/3218	16
Vase, 7½" bud/1905	10
Vase, 7½" handled/3103	20
Vase, 7½" flared/3217	16
Vase, 7½" oval/3220	18
Vase, 7½" milk can/canister/3688	20
Vase, 7½" flared/5135	12
Vase, 8" bud/4050	12
Vase, 9" oval/3264	20
Vase, 9" ribbed/3265	20
Vase, 9¾"/5023	25
Vase, double shell/3672	40

Green Lustre. Green Lustre has a chartreuse glaze under the 22-carat gold. The only listing I have seen is in the 1972 giftware price list.

Ash tray, oblong, 4¼"/1953	8
Ash tray, oblong, 6"/1954	8

Ash tray, oval, 8½″/3942	12
Ash tray, square, 9″/3915	16
Bowl, flower shape, 7″/3410–7	20
Bowl, flower shape, 9″/3410–9	25
Bowl, oval, 11¼″/5115S	20
Candle holder, Cosmos, pr, 2½″/5138	28
Dish, apple, single/3785	12
Dish, apple, double/3784	16
Dish, footed shell, 3″/5213	22
Dish, pear, single/3783	12
Pitcher, 5¼″/4060	16
Vase, 4″ Tulip/5144	12
Vase, 7¼″ flared/3218	16
Vase, 7½″ bud/1905	12
Vase, 7½″ handled/3103	22
Vase, 7½″ milk can/canister/3688	22
Vase, 8″ bud/4050	12
Vase, 9¾″/5023	22

Platina. In 1961, Stangl introduced Platina, platinum dry-brushed over a gray body.

Ash tray, Cosmos, 5½″/4033	8
Ash tray, fluted, 5″/3898–5	8
Ash tray, fluted, 7″/3898–7	12
Ash tray, Leaf, 6″/4036	8
Ash tray, Leaf, 6½″/4034	8
Ash tray, round, 10″/3972	16
Ash tray, shell, 5½″/4037	8
Ash tray, square, 9″/3915	16
Ash tray, triangle, 7″/3904S	8
Bowl, 7″/5061	16
Bowl, 8″/4061	16
Bowl, 9½″/5062	25
Bowl, 10¼″/4062	22
Bowl, ruffled, 10″/4084	30
Candle holder, 2″/5069	30
Candle holder, 3″/5070	30
Candle holder, ruffled, footed, 3⅞″/4083	30
Cigarette box, fluted	22
Compote, 6½″ (1388)/4021	20
Compote, 7″/5063	22
Compote, 9½″/5064	30
Horn of Plenty, 7¼″/5065	22
Horn of Plenty, 10″/5066	35
Planter, Swan, 5″/5034	20
Planter, Swan, 6¾″/5033	20
Planter, Swan, 9¾″/5032	30
Shell, 7½″/4018	12
Shell, 9⅛″/4019	16

Shell, 10½″/4020	20
Vase, 5⅛″/4004	12
Vase, 9¼″/5037	30
Vase, 9¾″/5023	25

MEDITERRANEAN A cobalt blue and dark green sponged finish.

Ash tray, 7¼″/5058	22
Ash tray, 11¼″ diameter/4026	30
Ash tray, Cosmos, 5½″/4033	15
Ash tray, leaf, 6″ x 4½″/4036	15
Ash tray, leaf, 6½″ x 4″/4034	15
Ash tray, oblong, 6½″ x 4½″/5097	15
Ash tray, oblong, 12½″ x 6½″/5004	30
Ash tray, oval, 8½″ x 7″/3942	22
Ash tray, round, 8½″ diameter/3973	22
Ash tray, round, 10″/3972	30
Ash tray, safety, 7¼″ x 6¼″/3977M	15
Ash tray, shell, 5″ x 5½″/4037	15
Ash tray, square, 9″/3915	30
Bowl, 8″/4061	40
Bowl, 8¼″/3980	30
Bowl, 10¼″/4062	40
Bowl, Cosmos, 12″/5139	45
Bowl, footed, 9″/4028	50
Candle holder, pair, 2″/5069	50
Cigarette set (box & 2 trays, 5″)/3898C	70
Compote, 6½″ x 3½″ (1388)/4021	30
Dish, apple, single/3785	22
Dish, apple, double/3784	30
Dish, pear, single/3783	22
Dish, pear, double/3782	30
Horn of Plenty, 4½″ x 7¼″/5065	38
Horn of Plenty, 6½″ x 10″/5066	50
Pitcher, 5¼″/4060	30
Pitcher, 6¼″/4059	38
Pitcher, 8¼″/4056	30
Pitcher, 11¼″/4055	38
Pitcher, 12″/4053	45
Shell, 7½″ wide/4018	22
Swan, 5″ high/5034	35
Tray, Ivy Leaf, 8″ x 7¾″/5146	22
Urn, 6″/3987	30
Vase, 9¾″/5023	38
Vase, bud, 5¾″/5093	15
Vase, bud, 8″/4050	30
Vase, flared, 7½″/5135	22
Vase, flared, 10½″/5132	40

PEBBLESTONE Developed by Kay Hackett. "Carefree natural pebble texture available in flowing earth tones of Amber, Jade or Blue." The line used the three basic Terra Rose colors.

Kay Hackett: "I did the experimenting to work that up. These were materials they had in the shop and I was trying to do something else with [them]. You have a red clay piece with an engobe. You take a wide brush and you spin on one of three colors, either manganese brown, cobalt blue or copper green. And then you take this satin glaze and sponge this on top, just place it carefully. It was easy to overdo or underdo. Then it was fired [a second time] and that kind of ran into the [color] and gave this mottled effect."

Ash tray, 7¼″ diameter/5271	20
Ash tray, 8″ x 10½″/3926	25
Bowl, 9″/3983	30
Bud vase, 6¾″/3981	25
Bud vase, 9¼″/4049	35
Candle holder, tapered, 7½″ diameter/5272	30
Candle holder, 5″ diameter/5273	25
Candy dish, round, squat, 7″ diameter/5270	30
Centerpiece, 14¼″/3774	35
Tray, oval, 11″ x 4¼″/5115–S	30
Urn, 13″/3993	50
Vase, 6¾″/4007	25
Vase, 8½″/5274	35
Vase, 9″/3979	35
Vase, 15″/3999	50

Stangl

PEBBLESTONE GIFTWARE

5274

5270

3993

3774

5272

4007

5273

5115-S

3926

3983

4049

3981

3999

5271

3979

STANGL POTTERY • P.O. BOX 2080 • TRENTON, NEW JERSEY 08607

111

MUGS

Stangl introduced two lines of mugs in the thirties.

CHARACTER MUGS/PITCHERS Glazed in light brown or light green with ivory caricature. Roosevelt's theme song, "Happy Days Are Here Again," is on the reverse of the pitcher.

Fred Israel, political historian, researched the men whose faces adorn this set and discovered that the element they had in common was their involvement with the Democratic national convention of 1932.

Under the party rules of the time, Roosevelt needed two-thirds of the delegate vote to be the nominee. John Nance Garner, Texan and Speaker of the House, desired the presidency. He was supported by William Randolph Hearst (both were opposed to the U.S. joining the League of Nations, as was Roosevelt). However, Garner and his supporters were more opposed to the other potential nominee, Alfred Smith, than to Roosevelt.

Smith, Governor of New York, was the favorite of a conservative group of Democrats who opposed Roosevelt and hoped to deadlock the convention with the Smith candidacy, and then nominate a dark horse.

Candidates for this dark horse nomination were Newton D. Baker, former Secretary of War under Wilson, in favor of the U.S. joining the League of Nations, and Albert Ritchie, conservative and popular four-term governor of Maryland.

On the first ballot, Roosevelt fell short of the two-thirds needed, though he was leading Al Smith, and Garner placed third with the help of California Senator Wm. McAdoo, later Sec'y of the Treasury, who kept California in the Garner camp. After the third ballot, everyone thought the convention was deadlocked and that Baker would be the candidate.

James Farley, Roosevelt's campaign manager (later Postmaster General) had a strategy. The Texas delegation was key. He spoke with Texas congressman Sam Rayburn and promised Garner the vice-presidency in exchange for his support. Next, Joseph Kennedy called Hearst and warned him that if he didn't support Roosevelt, he'd get Baker.

Finally, Garner, who didn't want the vice-presidency ("It's not worth a pitcher of warm piss"), was persuaded by McAdoo, Rayburn, Hearst and other backers not to deadlock the convention and let Baker get the nomination. Roosevelt won on the fourth ballot.

Knowing who these men are and what they did does not answer the question of why these mugs were made, or for whom; if it was a special order, who ordered them?

Because of the odd number of mugs, the existence of an eighth has been proposed. But given the abundance of Roosevelt mugs compared with the others, it is possible that two sets

Mugs, left to right: *Roosevelt, Garner, Smith, McAdoo, and Farley.* Center, *Roosevelt jug. Reproduction makes mugs look much darker than they are.*

were offered: the jug and six Roosevelts or the jug and the six others.

Pricing. Green is harder to find; add 10% to the prices listed.

1647–1	Pitcher, Franklin Delano Roosevelt	300
1647–1	Mug, Franklin Delano Roosevelt	75
1647–2	Mug, John Nance Garner	100
1647–3	Mug, Alfred Smith	125
1647–4	Mug, Wm. Gibbs McAdoo	100
1647–5	Mug, Albert Ritchie	100
1647–6	Mug, Newton D. Baker	100
1647–7	Mug, James Farley	100

STOBY MUGS (1936) Designed by Tony Sarg. The hat (lid) serves as an ashtray for six of the mugs. Batch and Grand have attached hats.

The Stobies were originally issued with hand-painted natural features (also, a Colonial Blue mug from this period has been seen). The six with separate lids were reissued in the 1970s in solid colors of brown with black trim, chartreuse or yellow. Depression's name was changed to Cry Baby.

An unlisted Stoby has turned up (see color section) with a space in the mouth that looks

Ritchie and Baker mugs.

like it would take a cigarette, so he is provisionally being called "Smoke." His hat has not yet been found.

Pricing. Prices are for mugs with correct hat. Expect to pay less if it is a marriage. For the reissues, price the brown at $100–125, and the chartreuse or yellow at $75–100.

Archie, 6½"/1681	200
Batch, 5"/1679	250
Chief, 6"/1676	250
Depression (Cry Baby), 5"/1677	200
Grand, 5"/1673	225
Henpeck, 6¼"/1680	225
Parson, 6½"/1675	200
"Smoke"/1674	ND
Sport, 5½"/1678	225

POTPOURRI

This chapter covers popular and unusual items that don't fit anywhere else in the book.

THE AMERICAN WAY PRODUCTS The American Way was a sales organization that handled a variety of products (glass, pottery, fabrics, were some) from dozens of manufacturers. Stangl provided three lines: Terra Rose artware in Amethyst, an exclusive color; and two lines of dinnerware (Clover is illustrated). Designers Petra Cabot and Douglas Meier were brought in for the project. Not many of these pieces show up.

Pricing. Price the Terra Rose Amethyst the same as the other colors, and use Garden Flower prices for the dinnerware.

DEALER SIGNS The gold and silver signs are the most common and go for around $50. On all other signs, it is a seller's market.

"DECO DELIGHT" A vase has been reported but not confirmed. It may be the Deco vase (see Rainbow Ware) that is very similar.

Creamer	50
Cup	20
Lamp	ND
Plate, 7¼" x 6¼"	35
Plate, party, 7¼" x 6¼"	45
Saucer	10
Sugar	75
Teapot	150

PITCHER AND BOWL SETS These were hand-painted (not carved) with pink roses or blue violets (the New Jersey state flower). AD cups and saucers with pink roses have been found.

Bowl, 12"	60
Bowl, 15"	75
Pitcher, 9" tall	60
Pitcher, 11" tall	75

SALAD SETS Stangl used salad sets (also called short sets) to test the market for new pat-

The American Way Leaf plate and Clover individual casserole.

"Deco Delight" sugar, lamp (first one seen), cup and teapot.

Violets pitcher and Antique Rose bowl.

Lemon

Lime

Pheasant

"Shooting Star"

Songbird

Kumquat

Wind Fall

Black Olive

terns. If they proved popular with the buying public, as did Fruit, for example, they were expanded into dinnerware sets. If not, they were discontinued, which explains why some of these patterns are hard to find.

There is no hard-and-fast rule about what items you will find in these sets. Though the basic salad set is a 10″ salad bowl, 14″ chop plate and six 8″ plates, you will also find cups and sau-

cers and more. Kay Hackett: "Well, it [cups and saucers and other pieces] would be something they would add as they went along . . . they would add things if there was a demand for them. The salesman might say, well, so and so store will accept this if this [an additional item] is added to it. So we'd make them up."

In addition, oval salads with raised rims and five-sided chop plates were tried for Kumquat and Lime, but they proved to be too expensive to produce.

Known decorations are: Appletree, Banquet (a fruit pattern), Black Olive, Blossom Time, Fig, Fish (Turquoise), Fish (Yellow), Gooseberry, Kumquat, Lime, Pheasant, "Shooting Star," Songbird and Wind Fall (large maple leaves). You will not find every pattern on all pieces listed here. #1940, a three-piece set with raised fruit, is found in natural colors as well as the four Tropical Ware colors.

Pricing. Prices are for all patterns except Pheasant and Songbird, which are Not Determined.

Bowl, salad, oval, 11½ x 10½"	50
Bowl, salad, round, 10"	35
Creamer	12
Cup	10
Plate, 8"	15
Plate, 9"	20
Plate, 10"	25
Plate, chop, 12"	30
Plate, chop, 14"	40
Plate, chop, 5-sided	60
Plate, chop, square, 12"	50
Saucer	5
Sugar	18

WIG AND HAT STANDS   These were based on an idea that Mr. Stangl had. Initially, they were made exclusively for a wig store in New York. Later they were available to other stores and at retail.

They stand 15" tall, with a head size of 22½". Firsts are on a square wooden base with the name "Stangl" burned into the sides. Seconds, which were sold at Flemington, are on round pottery bases. Some wigstands were made into lamp bases.

All were hand painted by Irene Sarnecki. The women are blonde or brunette; blondes are harder to find. Shades will vary; some are almost redheads. The man is very hard to find. Irene Sarnecki: "There weren't many. They decided to try it for men who wore toupees. I don't think it went over too well. Because at that time men were a lot more vain than they are today. They don't want this sitting [around]." Some plain white wig stands were also sold.

Only fifty of these ash trays were made for a special New Jersey state occasion. Each one was hand signed by Governor Brendan Byrne.

Wig stands.

Pricing. The stand for the man is ND; for the woman, $225–$250.

SMOKING LINES

A number of sets and individual smoking items were made over the years by Stangl.

ASH TRAYS/CARD SUITS There are four shapes: club, diamond, heart and spade. These will be found in standard 1930s glazes, as well as later glazes of chartreuse, dark green, off-pink and white. Some may be found in Fulper glazes.

30s glazes	10–15
New glazes	8–10

ASH TRAY/CIGARETTE BOX SETS (1942) There are two basic styles of cigarette boxes in these sets: square and rectangular. A set consisted of one box and two ash trays. These sets are found in many of the dinnerware decorations; I am covering only the non-dinnerware decorations here.

Kay Hackett: "A friend of mine had been to Hawaii and she loaned a great book with shell ginger and hibiscus and so forth." This was the basis for six boxes one year.

The first six decorations to appear were: Daisy/3666, Floral/3636, Heart/3638, Star & Flower/3631, Tulip/3630 (same as dinnerware) and Tulip & Buds/3665. Other known decorations are:

Apple Tree/3845
Baltimore Oriole/3934
Blossom Time/3886
Bluebird/3936
Brown Wren w/Yellow Tulip/3840
Butterfly/3802
Dogwood/3796
Flower Buds/3792
Flower/3801
Fruit/3798
Gladiola/3794
Goldfinch/3843
Goldfinch/3931
Grape/3800
Harlequin/3907
Humming Bird/3842
Ivy/3797
Marsh Rose/3799
Poppies/3885
Prothonatary Warbler/3932
Purple Finch/3933
Rhododendron/3841
Rose Bud
Scarlet Tanager/3935
Single Bird
Trillium /3793
Tropic Flower/3791
Trumpet Flower/3795
Yellow Iris

Ash Trays. The basic ash tray is round, 5″ diameter. These are the same shape as the coaster/ash trays sold with the dinnerware lines. You will also find 5″ ash trays that are roundish squares, 4½″ round and 4⅜″ square. The last two are mainly from the early forties.

Birds	20
Flowers	15
Ivy	10

Cigarette Boxes/Square. The basic box is 3¾″ x 4½″. Early boxes that measure 5″ x 4″ or 4″ x 3¼″ will also be found, as will a box with a pagoda-shaped lid. Known decorations on this latter box are: Butterfly, Flower, Fruit, Grape, Ivy and Marsh Rose.

Birds	60–75
Flowers	30–40
Ivy	25

Cigarette Boxes/Rectangular. All are 3⅜″ x 7¼″ and originally sold for $3.50. Known decorations are: Dogwood, Flower Buds, Gladiola, Trillium, Tropic Flower and Trumpet Flower.

Pricing. All patterns are $35–$40.

Top row: Tulip/3630; Star & Flower/3631; Floral/3636. Second row: Daisy/3666; Tulip & Buds/3665; Heart/3638. Third row: Apple Tree/3845; Baltimore Oriole/3934; Blossom Time/3886. Fourth row: Bluebird/3936; Brown Wren w/Yellow Tulip/3840; Butterfly/3802.

Top row: Dogwood/3796; Flower Buds/3792; Flower/3801. Second row: Fruit/3798; Gladiola/3794; Gold-finch/3843. Third row: Goldfinch/3931; Grape/3800; Humming Bird/3842. Fourth row: Ivy/3797; Marsh Rose/3799; Poppies/3885.

Top row: Prothonatary Warbler/3932; Purple Finch/3933; Rhododendron/3841. Second row: Rose Bud; Scarlet Tanager/3935; Single Bird. Third row: Trillium/3793; Tropic Flower/3791. Fourth row: Trumpet Flower/3795; Yellow Iris.

Left to right: Large Cosmos ash tray, small Cosmos ash tray, Pansy bowl, small Pansy ash tray, large Pansy ash tray, Poppy bowl, Tulip ash tray and Rose ash tray. Although the bowls are not part of the Smoking Line, I've included them here to show that they will be found with multicolored decoration.

ASH TRAYS/FLOWER   There are four shapes: Cosmos, Pansy, Rose and Tulip. Rose and Tulip are harder to find. Some of these may have been designed by Auguste Jacob.

Pricing. These are priced by color. Yellow and yellow-brown are at the low end of the range, solid colors are in the middle, and multicolors are at the high end of the range.

Cosmos, 3½″	8–15
Cosmos, 5½″	15–25
Pansy, 4″	8–15
Pansy, 6″	15–25
Pansy, bowl, 6″	25–35
Poppy, bowl, 4″	25–35
Rose, 4″	10–15
Rose bowl, 4″	25–35
Tulip, 4″	10–15

ASH TRAYS/LEAF   A variety of shapes and colors will be found. See also Terra Rose.

Pricing. All ash trays, $10–$12.

ASH TRAYS/OVAL   /3926

Fantasy	30–35
Radiant	30–35
Spectrum	30–35

ASH TRAYS/SQUARE   /3915 Kay Hackett: "This was a series [Pink Elephant] I did for New Year's plates. I don't think we ever produced any of these to speak of, maybe a few."

Big Top	50–60
Pink Elephant	50–60

Top row: Fantasy, Radiant, and Spectrum. Bottom: Big Top and Pink Elephant.

SPECIAL-ORDER ITEMS

Stangl made a large number of items for special orders. Sometimes it was a regular Stangl line with the customer's name stamped on the bottom, such as some Kiddie Ware. Jewelled Christmas Tree will be found stamped for Carole Stupell, a New York store. Also, a number of regular items will be found marked Resco, a company that gave them as Christmas gifts.

Irene Sarnecki: " We had a lot of different companies that sent things in and asked us to reproduce this for them as a company gift. As long as we had the time, and if it didn't take up that much time, and they were good at paying, that was the whole thing behind these special things."

Stangl also created exclusive designs. For Carbone, a distributor, they created Blue Mill, Pomona and Poppies.

FISHER, BRUCE/DELLA WARE   Della Ware was produced from the late thirties through the forties for Fisher, Bruce, a distributor located in Philadelphia. Martha Stangl, one of Martin's daughters, played a role in its naming, development and marketing.

#1902   White body. This shape has raised bands that are concentric on the flatware and horizontal on the hollowware.

The Beverage Set items (see Dinnerware/Early) and the miniature jug are not listed here, as they have not been found with Della Ware decorations.

The following decorations are hand-painted but not carved:

Rialto tea pot.

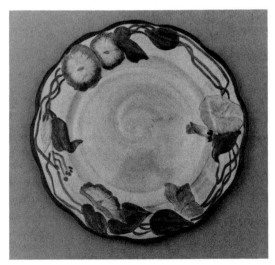

Morning Glories chop plate.

"Quimper" pattern bowl, the only piece known in this Della Ware pattern.

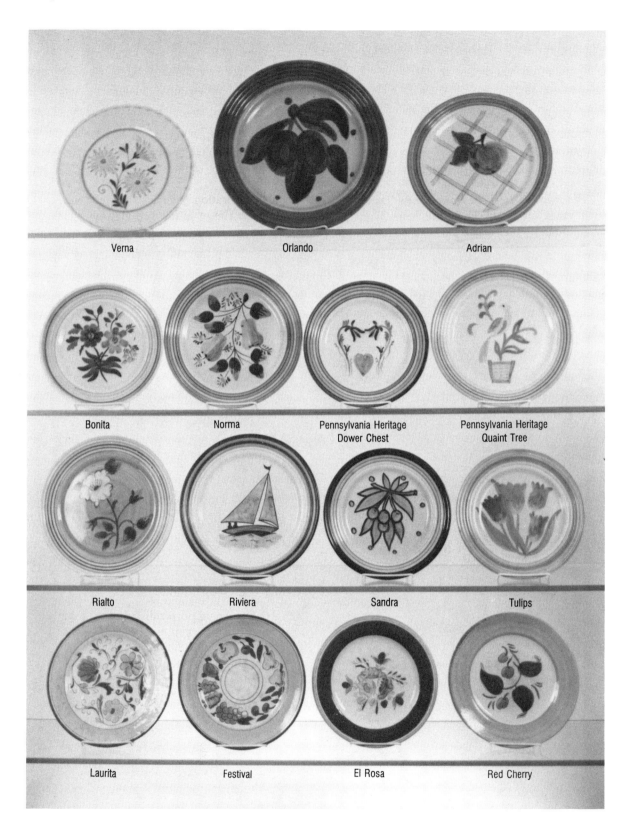

Verna Orlando Adrian

Bonita Norma Pennsylvania Heritage
Dower Chest Pennsylvania Heritage
Quaint Tree

Rialto Riviera Sandra Tulips

Laurita Festival El Rosa Red Cherry

Adrian   Red apple over plaid on white background. Do not confuse this with the stoneware Adrian pattern made for Altman's.

Bonita   Spray of pink, blue and yellow flowers on ivory background with multicolor rim.

Norma   Pink and yellow pears, blue flowers, green leaves.

Olivia   Blurry green plums.

Orlando   Brown plums and leaves on tan background with brown rim.

Pennsylvania Heritage Dower Chest   A Pennsylvania Dutch design: blue heart with blue, brown and green decoration.

Pennsylvania Heritage Quaint Tree   A bird on a tree in a flowerpot in colors of blue, green, red and yellow with multicolor rim.

Rialto   A yellow flower and green leaves on a medium blue background with yellow ribbing.

Riviera   Blue and white sailboat (similar to Newport).

Sandra   Green cherries and leaves outlined in blue with green and blue rim.

Tulips   Pastel shades.

Known pieces are:

Bowl, soup, coupe, 8″	15
Bowl, soup, lug	12
w/lid	18
Bowl, soup, rim	12
Bowl, vegetable, round, 9″	25
Bowl, vegetable, round, 10″	35
Candle holder	15
Carafe w/pottery stopper	85
Creamer	12
Cup	8
Plate, 6″	8
Plate, 8″	15
Plate, 10″	20
Plate, 11″	25
Plate, chop, 12½″	35
Saucer	3
Sugar	15
Teapot	60

#3434   In 1942, Stangl shifted its Della Ware production to a red body with carved decorations, as it did with its other dinnerware lines.

Four patterns have been found on Stangl's rimmed shape. El Rosa, Festival and Laurita were inspired by Italian designs that Martin Stangl brought to Kay Hackett and asked her to adapt.

El Rosa   (‹1942) Designed by Kay Hackett. A rose centered in a lavender and green floral, with a green and yellow rim.

Festival   (1942) Designed by Kay Hackett. A fruit decoration encircles the well, with a solid color rim of yellow and green.

Laurita   (‹1942) Designed by Kay Hackett. A triple flower motif, blue, red and yellow, with a rim of yellow and green.

Red Cherry   Red cherries, green leaves and gold rim.

Pricing. Use Garden Flower prices.

"Fluted Edge"

Verna/KH   Yellow chrysanthemums, green leaves on white background.

Pricing. Use #1902 prices.

Molded and Carved   Two lines of Della Ware were molded and carved:

Dogwood   (1943) Shape designed by Auguste Jacob. Pink flowers and green leaves. This is the same shape that is used for the Dogwoods in the Prestige line.

Morning Glories   Pink, blue and yellow flowers, twining vines.

Pricing. Use Garden Flower prices.

LUNNING   An importer/distributor. I have turned up little information. The story seems to be that the Second World War cut off Lunning's European sources of supply, and he turned to Stangl (if not others) to get pottery manufactured. How long this association lasted after the war ended is not clear; possibly through the end of the forties. (See also Kiddie Sets & Musical Mug in the Children's Ware section).

Known shapes and patterns are listed below. A set of #1388 in Terra Rose green has also been found.

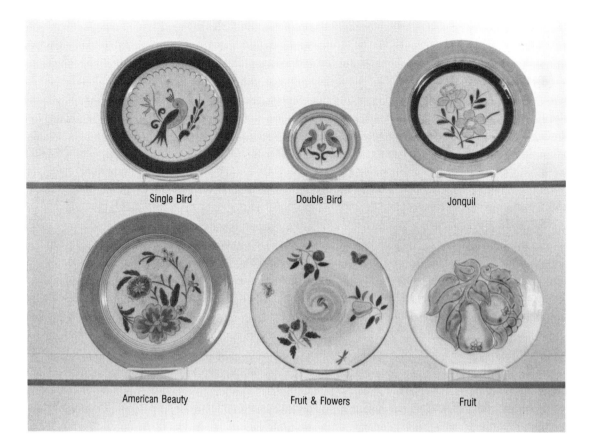

Single Bird   Double Bird   Jonquil

American Beauty   Fruit & Flowers   Fruit

#3434. The following patterns are all carved:

American Beauty   Spray of pink, blue and yellow flowers with wide blue rim.
Double Bird   Designed by Kay Hackett.
Fruit & Flowers   Designed by Kay Hackett. Small fruits, flowers and butterflies.
Jonquil   Yellow rim with a green stripe.
Single Bird   Designed by Kay Hackett.

Pricing. Use Garden Flower prices.

Molded "Fruit"   Molded fruit in the center of the plate, in Terra Rose/Mauve glaze.

Pricing. Use Salad Set prices.

PEACOCK   Kay Hackett: "There's a peacock plate. We made it for a jeweler in Chicago and his name was C.D. Peacock. It was designed for production but it was too difficult to be cost effective. I did a dozen fourteen-inch plates for Flemington and it was later adapted for the eleven-inch plate for Peacock and sold exclusively to him with his name hand written on the

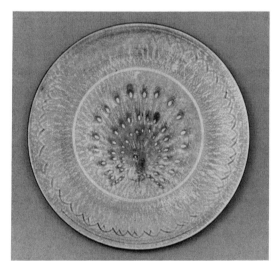

Peacock chop plate.

back in gold." The eleven-inch plate has a wide rim and the decoration in the center. Price is ND.

TIFFANY   It was a source of great pride for Stangl that Caughley was the first domestic pottery ever bought by Tiffany.

CAUGHLEY A sponged decoration that differs from Town and Country. Irene Sarnecki: "Town and Country had one coat of paint, whereas [Caughley], you would put a light coat of that color underneath covering the entire [piece], front and back, then you would come back with the same color but using it a little heavier to give you a double tone but it was completely covered, you showed no white. And that was the difference between the two."

The butter bottom, gravy liner and oval snack tray are the same piece. The soup bowl is called a cream soup in Caughley flyers but it is a regular soup, not the traditional two-handled shape.

You will find Blue, Brown, Green, Honey, Pink and Yellow, although Honey and Pink may not have been put on every item. Olde Glory—red and blue sponged over white—was introduced in 1976 for the U.S. Bicentennial; Olde Vermont (brown and yellow) was introduced the same year; although it is in the Caughley literature, it has the Stangl mark, not the Tiffany.

Pricing. The "Others" column includes Brown, Green, Honey, Pink, Yellow and Olde Vermont. Olde Glory is ND.

	Blue	Others
Baking dish, 1½ quart	60	40
Baking dish, 2½ quart	85	60
Bowl, salad, round, 3 quart, 10″	50	35
Bowl, salad, round, 4 quart, 12″	65	40
Bowl, soup, 8″	25	15
Bowl, vegetable, round, 1½ quart, 8″	40	25
Butter, ¼ pound	50	35
Candlestick, 7½″	85	50
Casserole, 2 quart	55	40
Casserole, 3 quart	65	50
Coffee pot, 6 cup	75	55
Creamer	20	15
Cup, 9 ounce	15	10
Dish, soup/cereal, 20 ounce, 6″	25	15
Flower pot, 5″	30	20
Flower pot, 6″	35	25
Flower pot, 7½″	45	35
Ginger jar	85	60
Gravy	40	25
Gravy liner	25	15
Jug, 1 quart	40	25
Jug, 2 quart	65	45
Mold, fluted, 6″	50	35
Mug, 13 ounce	35	25
Pie baker, 11″	50	35
Plate, 6″	8	6
Plate, 8¼″	12	10
Plate, 10⅝″	20	15
Plate, chop, 12″	35	30
Platter, oval, 11¾″	35	25
Platter, oval, 15″	50	35
Saucer	5	3
Shaker, cylinder	15	10
Sugar	25	20
Teapot, 4 cup	65	50
Tray, relish, 7½″	25	20
Tray, snack, oval, 8¼″	25	15
Tureen, 4-piece (bottom, lid, ladle and tray), 3½ quart	300	225

SPORTSMEN'S GIFTWARE

Introduced in the mid-forties, made through the early sixties at least. The square ash tray was made with either a round well or a square well. Cigarette boxes were sold individually or with two ash trays, the 5" round ones which doubled as coasters.

The golfer ash trays came with a ceramic golf ball in the center; you could knock your pipe against it to clean the ashes. If the ball fell off in the kiln, the space was ground down and the ash tray was sold plain.

Most of these decorations are on a gray background.

Ash tray, boomerang/3927
California Quail	45–50
Pine	35
Sailfish	50–60
Tropical (fish)	50–60
Woodcock	45–50

Ash tray, oval, 10⅝"/3926
Blue Wing Teal	45–50
California Quail	45–50
Canada Goose	35–40
Deer	45–50
Duck (Mallard)	35–40
Golfer	60
w/golf ball	75
Green Wing Teal	45–50
Partridge	45–50
Pheasant	35
Pintail	45–50
Quail	45–50
Ruffed Grouse	45–50
Sailfish	50–60
Striped Bass	50–60
Woodcock	45–50
Wood Duck	45–50

Ash tray, round, fluted rim, 7"/3898
(sold as a set)
Canada Goose	25–30
Flying Duck	25–30
Mallard	25–30
Pheasant	25–30

Ash tray, round, 8¼"
Deer	45–50
Fish	45–50
Flying Duck	45–50

Hunting Dog	45–50
Pheasant	45–50
Sailfish	45–50

Ash tray, square, square well, 9"/3914
Coral	20–25
Gray	20–25
White	20–25

Ash tray, square, round well, 9"/3915
Canvasback	50
Caribbean	60
Golfer w/ball	75
Mallard	50
Porpoise	60
Rainbow Trout	60
Redhead	50

Cigarette box, 3¾ x 4½"
Canada Goose	75–85
Flying Duck	75–85
Mallard	75–85
Pheasant	75–85

Coaster, 5"/5011
Canada Goose	25–30
Flying Duck	25–30
Mallard	25–30
Pheasant	25–30

Mug, 1 cup
Hunter	25

Mug, 2 cup
Canada Goose	35
Flying Duck	35
Mallard	35
Pheasant	35

Plate, 11"/3774, white or gray background.
Canada Goose	50
Canvasback	50
Mallard	50
Pheasant	50
Quail	50
Wood Duck	50

Plate, 14½"/3774
Pheasant	75–100

129

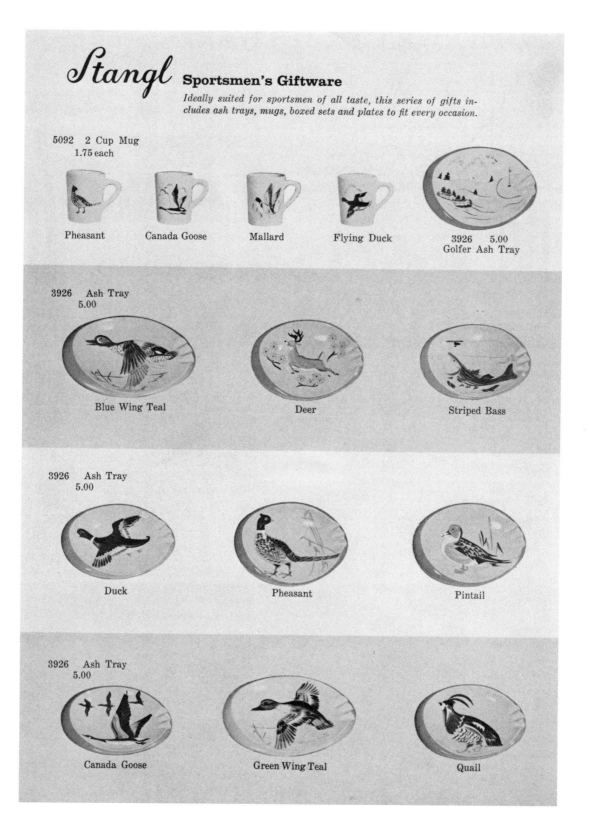

Stangl **Sportsmen's Giftware**

Ideally suited for sportsmen of all taste, this series of gifts includes ash trays, mugs, boxed sets and plates to fit every occasion.

5092   2 Cup Mug
1.75 each

Pheasant   Canada Goose   Mallard   Flying Duck

3926   5.00
Golfer Ash Tray

3926   Ash Tray
5.00

Blue Wing Teal   Deer   Striped Bass

3926   Ash Tray
5.00

Duck   Pheasant   Pintail

3926   Ash Tray
5.00

Canada Goose   Green Wing Teal   Quail

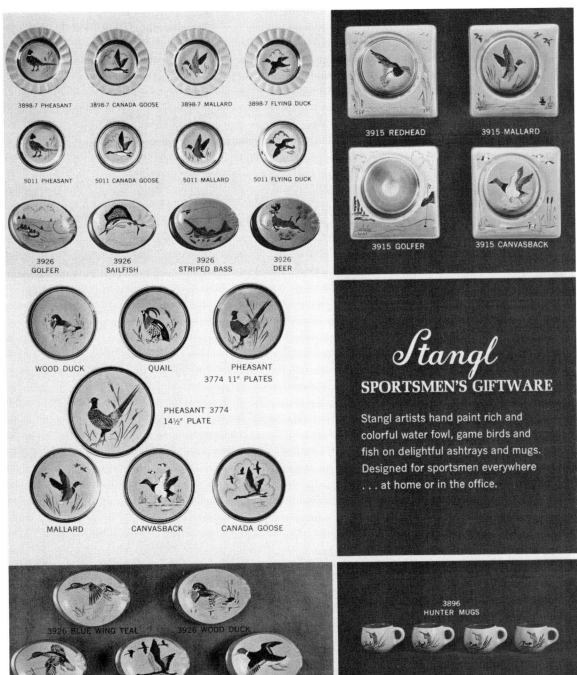

3898-7 PHEASANT   3898-7 CANADA GOOSE   3898-7 MALLARD   3898-7 FLYING DUCK

5011 PHEASANT   5011 CANADA GOOSE   5011 MALLARD   5011 FLYING DUCK

3926 GOLFER   3926 SAILFISH   3926 STRIPED BASS   3926 DEER

3915 REDHEAD   3915 MALLARD

3915 GOLFER   3915 CANVASBACK

WOOD DUCK   QUAIL   PHEASANT

3774 11" PLATES

PHEASANT 3774
14½" PLATE

MALLARD   CANVASBACK   CANADA GOOSE

Stangl
SPORTSMEN'S GIFTWARE

Stangl artists hand paint rich and colorful water fowl, game birds and fish on delightful ashtrays and mugs. Designed for sportsmen everywhere . . . at home or in the office.

3926 BLUE WING TEAL   3926 WOOD DUCK

3926 GREEN WING TEAL   3926 CANADA GOOSE   3926 DUCK

3926 PHEASANT   3926 PINTAIL   3926 QUAIL

3896
HUNTER MUGS

5092 PHEASANT   5092 FLYING DUCK   5092 CANADA GOOSE   5092 MALLARD

Bibliography

Blasberg, Robert W., *Fulper Art Pottery: An Aesthetic Appreciation 1909–1929.* Jordan-Volpe Gallery, 475 West Broadway, New York, NY 10012. 1979. Soft cover, 8½″ x 11″, 88 pages. No prices. Color section, black and white throughout. This book was also the gallery exhibit catalog. [Out of Print]

Evans, Paul, *Art Pottery of the United States.* Feingold & Lewis Publishing, 1088 Madison Avenue, New York, NY 10028. $45.00 + $2.00 p&h. No prices. Color section; photos throughout.

Stangl Pottery Company, various documents.

Matching Services

Popkorn (anything made by Stangl), 4 Mine Street, Flemington, NJ 08822. 908.782.9631. Popkorn will keep a list of your Stangl wants and notify you when they have found something.

Replacements (dinnerware only), 1089 Knox Road, Greensboro, NC 27420. Will send you a list of what they have in stock.

Clubs

Stangl Bird Collectors Association, c/o Diana Weigand, 325 West Upper Ferry Road, Apt. C-2, Trenton, NJ 08628. The club has a quarterly newsletter and two annual events: an auction in the spring, and a swap-and-sell in the fall. May expand to include all Stangl pottery.

Shape Library

This section has been assembled from current photographs and line drawings taken from old catalogs. It is here for purposes of identification and is meant to be used in conjunction with the line drawings and advertising reprints throughout the book.

It is not intended to be complete; it couldn't be. For one thing, the catalogs from which the line drawings were taken seem to have been produced only from 1935 to 1942.

When you put together as complete a list as possible, many numbers are missing. Some numbers were used for patterns, some for sets; one number was used for related pieces, such as the #1388 and #2000 dinnerware, or two or many shapes have just not turned up. And Stangl's numbering practices vary. Sometimes more sizes of the same shape, such as the #1792 flower pot. Other times, two different sizes of the same shape might have two consecutive numbers, such as the Pie Crust bowls #1741 and #1742. And several early items were re-numbered for the gold and silver giftware lines.

Finally, a word about console sets. You will find several in this section, most identified because the bowl and candleholder have consecutive numbers. Others don't, and while some are related by shape design, some aren't. For the record, some of these sets are: #1740 bowl/#1575 candleholder; #2064 bowl/#2059 candleholder; #3082 bowl/#3099 candleholder; #3083 bowl/#3087 candleholder; #3084 bowl/#3108 candleholder.

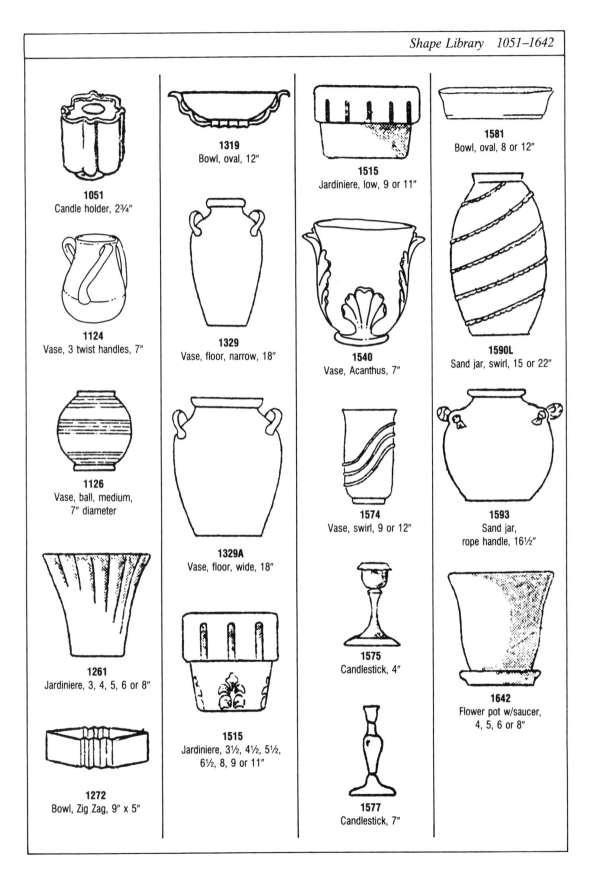

1051
Candle holder, 2¾″

1124
Vase, 3 twist handles, 7″

1126
Vase, ball, medium,
7″ diameter

1261
Jardiniere, 3, 4, 5, 6 or 8″

1272
Bowl, Zig Zag, 9″ x 5″

1319
Bowl, oval, 12″

1329
Vase, floor, narrow, 18″

1329A
Vase, floor, wide, 18″

1515
Jardiniere, 3½, 4½, 5½,
6½, 8, 9 or 11″

1515
Jardiniere, low, 9 or 11″

1540
Vase, Acanthus, 7″

1574
Vase, swirl, 9 or 12″

1575
Candlestick, 4″

1577
Candlestick, 7″

1581
Bowl, oval, 8 or 12″

1590L
Sand jar, swirl, 15 or 22″

1593
Sand jar,
rope handle, 16½″

1642
Flower pot w/saucer,
4, 5, 6 or 8″

133

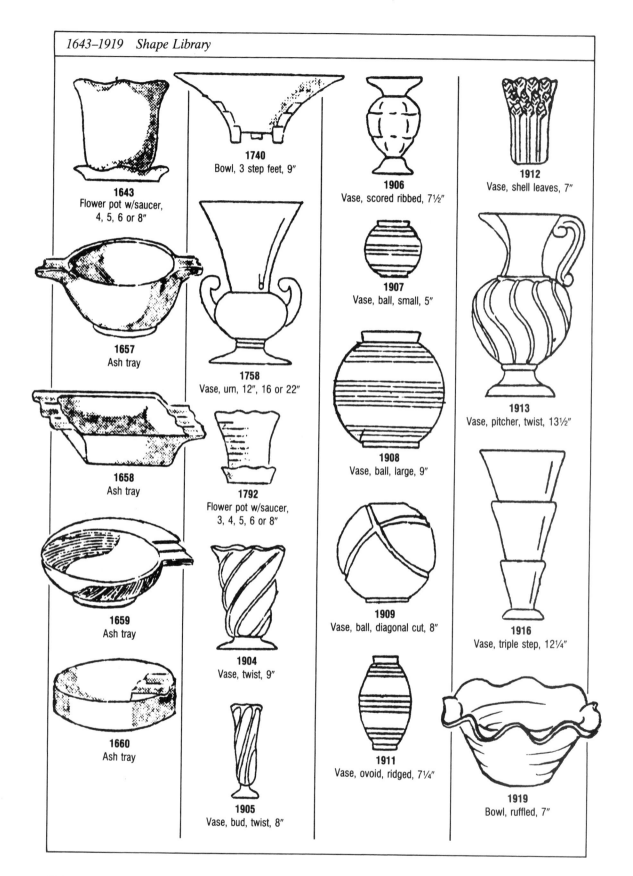

1643
Flower pot w/saucer,
4, 5, 6 or 8″

1657
Ash tray

1658
Ash tray

1659
Ash tray

1660
Ash tray

1740
Bowl, 3 step feet, 9″

1758
Vase, urn, 12″, 16 or 22″

1792
Flower pot w/saucer,
3, 4, 5, 6 or 8″

1904
Vase, twist, 9″

1905
Vase, bud, twist, 8″

1906
Vase, scored ribbed, 7½″

1907
Vase, ball, small, 5″

1908
Vase, ball, large, 9″

1909
Vase, ball, diagonal cut, 8″

1911
Vase, ovoid, ridged, 7¼″

1912
Vase, shell leaves, 7″

1913
Vase, pitcher, twist, 13½″

1916
Vase, triple step, 12¼″

1919
Bowl, ruffled, 7″

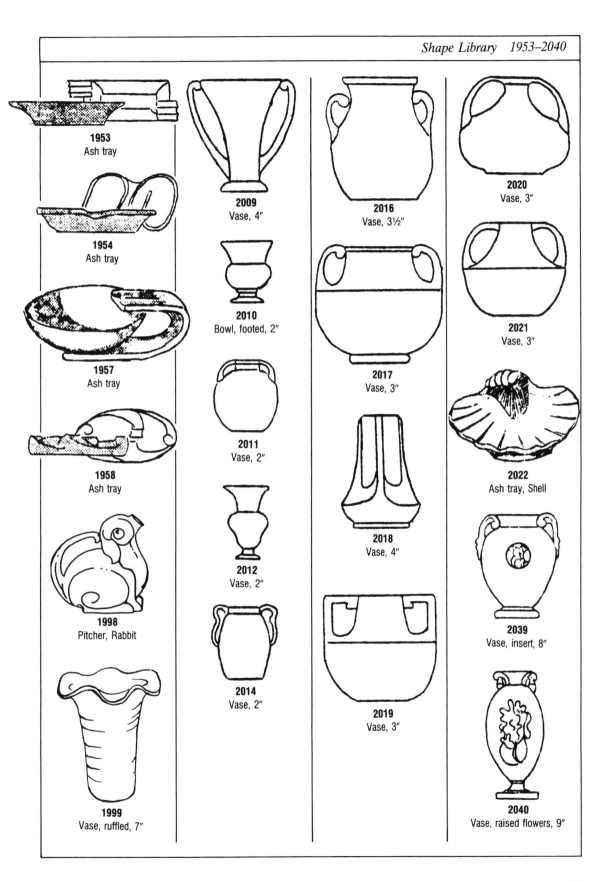

1953
Ash tray

1954
Ash tray

1957
Ash tray

1958
Ash tray

1998
Pitcher, Rabbit

1999
Vase, ruffled, 7″

2009
Vase, 4″

2010
Bowl, footed, 2″

2011
Vase, 2″

2012
Vase, 2″

2014
Vase, 2″

2016
Vase, 3½″

2017
Vase, 3″

2018
Vase, 4″

2019
Vase, 3″

2020
Vase, 3″

2021
Vase, 3″

2022
Ash tray, Shell

2039
Vase, insert, 8″

2040
Vase, raised flowers, 9″

135

2041
Vase, scroll handles,
square base, 8″

2042
Vase, Wheat, 8″

2043
Vase, scroll handle, 9″

2047
Vase, twist, 3 balls, 4½″

2048
Vase, 2 handle,
square base, 4½″

2050
Bowl, scallop, round, 8″

2051
Candle holder, scallop,
round, 2½″

2052
Vase, round scallop, 9½″

2053
Bowl, 3 footed, 12″

2054
Candle holder, double,
6½″ high

2055
Candle holder, double,
5½″ high

2056
Vase, scroll horn, 6″

2057
Vase, flower jar, oblong,
10″ x 4″

2058
Candle holder, oblong

2059
Candle holder, 4″

2060
Bowl, cradle, 7″ x 4″

2061
Candle holder, cradle

2062
Bowl, pointed, 9″

2063
Candle holder,
pointed, 3½″

2064
Bowl, scallop, oval, 9″

2065
Vase, cylinder,
ornamental, 9″

2066
Vase, capital, 8″

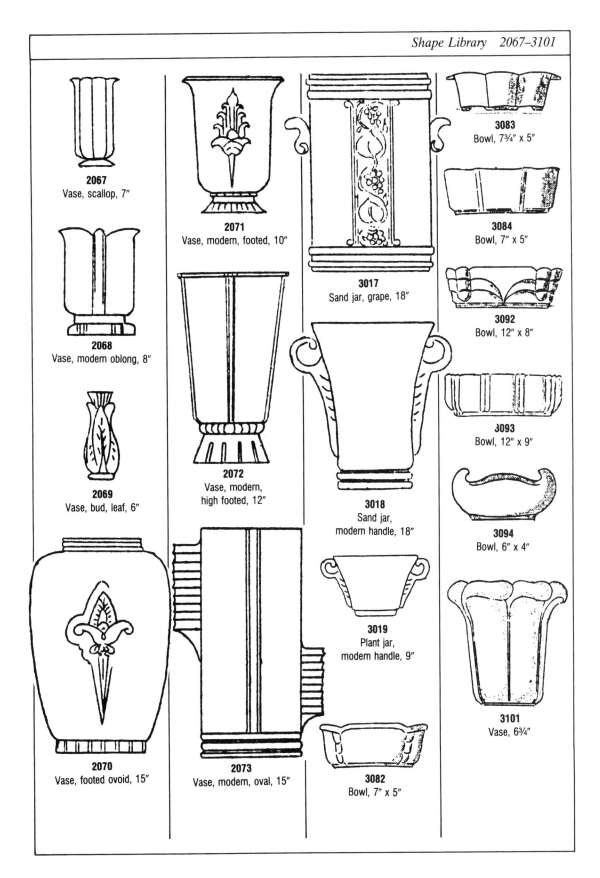

2067
Vase, scallop, 7″

2068
Vase, modern oblong, 8″

2069
Vase, bud, leaf, 6″

2070
Vase, footed ovoid, 15″

2071
Vase, modern, footed, 10″

2072
Vase, modern, high footed, 12″

2073
Vase, modern, oval, 15″

3017
Sand jar, grape, 18″

3018
Sand jar, modern handle, 18″

3019
Plant jar, modern handle, 9″

3082
Bowl, 7″ x 5″

3083
Bowl, 7¾″ x 5″

3084
Bowl, 7″ x 5″

3092
Bowl, 12″ x 8″

3093
Bowl, 12″ x 9″

3094
Bowl, 6″ x 4″

3101
Vase, 6¾″

137

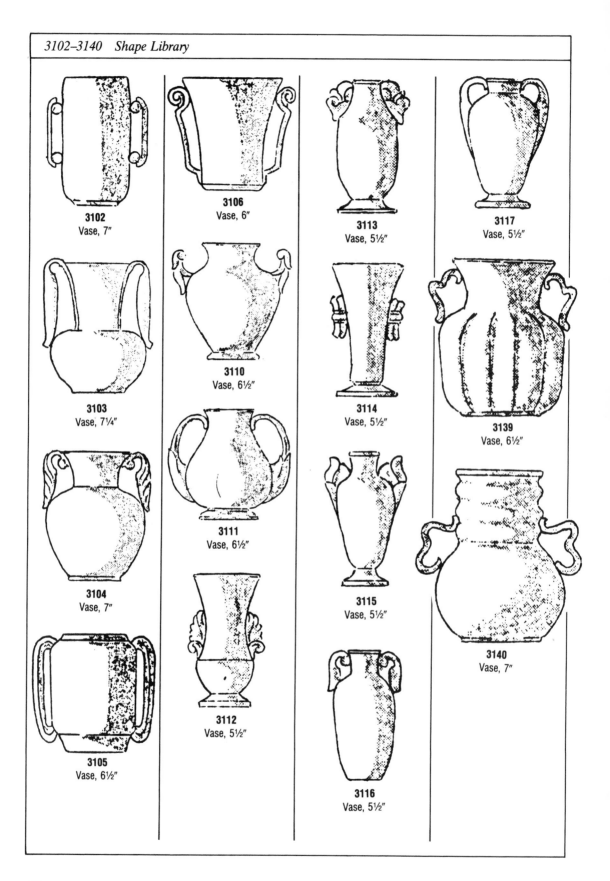

3102
Vase, 7″

3106
Vase, 6″

3113
Vase, 5½″

3117
Vase, 5½″

3103
Vase, 7¼″

3110
Vase, 6½″

3114
Vase, 5½″

3139
Vase, 6½″

3104
Vase, 7″

3111
Vase, 6½″

3115
Vase, 5½″

3140
Vase, 7″

3105
Vase, 6½″

3112
Vase, 5½″

3116
Vase, 5½″

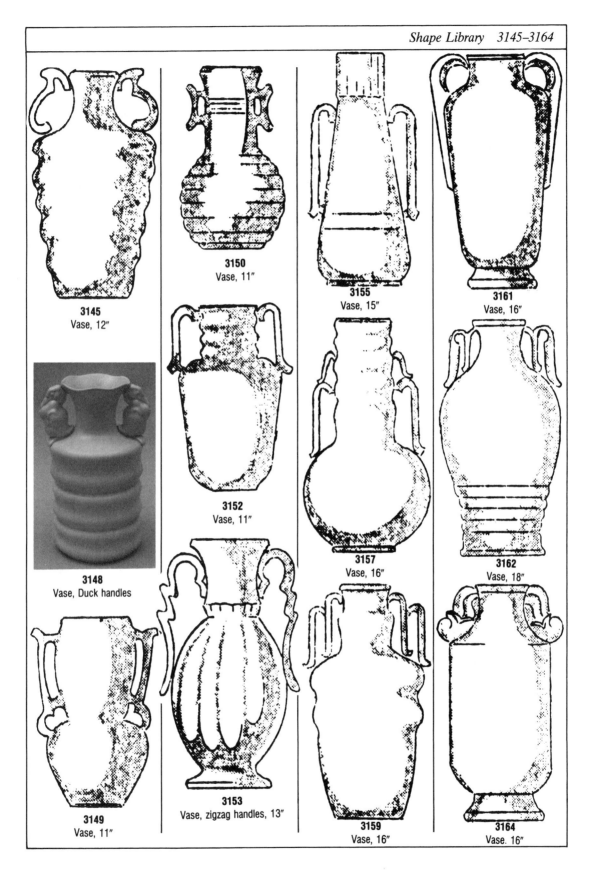

3145
Vase, 12″

3150
Vase, 11″

3155
Vase, 15″

3161
Vase, 16″

3148
Vase, Duck handles

3152
Vase, 11″

3157
Vase, 16″

3162
Vase, 18″

3149
Vase, 11″

3153
Vase, zigzag handles, 13″

3159
Vase, 16″

3164
Vase. 16″

139

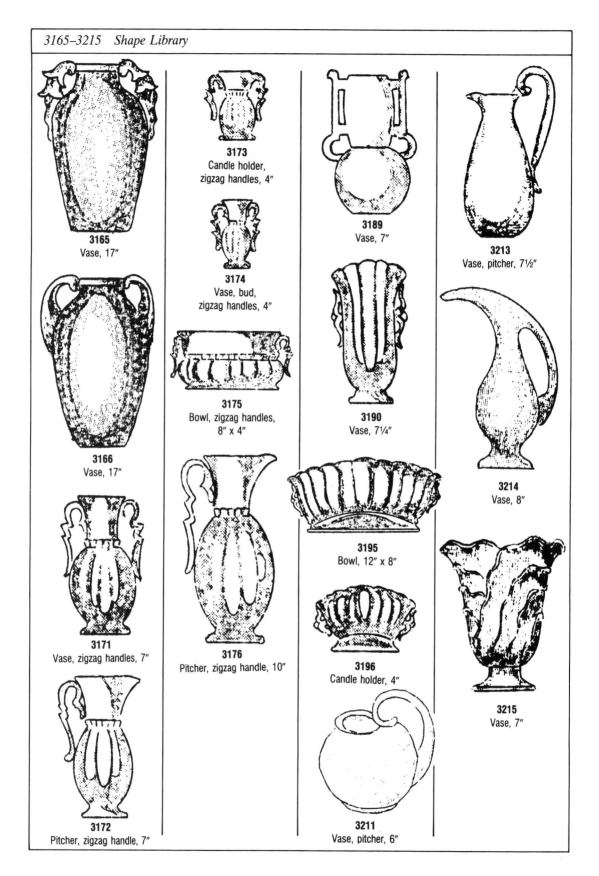

3165
Vase, 17″

3173
Candle holder,
zigzag handles, 4″

3174
Vase, bud,
zigzag handles, 4″

3189
Vase, 7″

3213
Vase, pitcher, 7½″

3166
Vase, 17″

3175
Bowl, zigzag handles,
8″ x 4″

3190
Vase, 7¼″

3171
Vase, zigzag handles, 7″

3176
Pitcher, zigzag handle, 10″

3195
Bowl, 12″ x 8″

3214
Vase, 8″

3196
Candle holder, 4″

3172
Pitcher, zigzag handle, 7″

3211
Vase, pitcher, 6″

3215
Vase, 7″

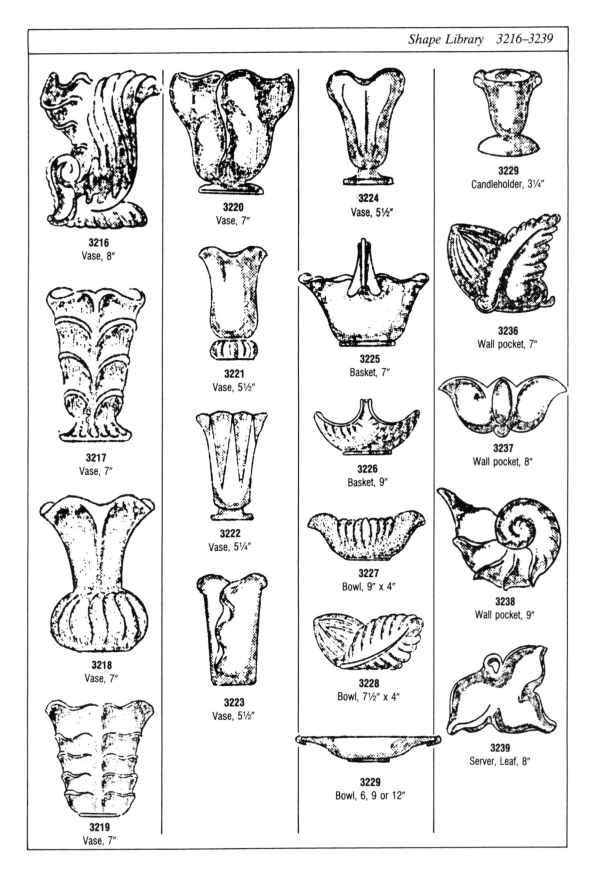

3216
Vase, 8″

3217
Vase, 7″

3218
Vase, 7″

3219
Vase, 7″

3220
Vase, 7″

3221
Vase, 5½″

3222
Vase, 5¼″

3223
Vase, 5½″

3224
Vase, 5½″

3225
Basket, 7″

3226
Basket, 9″

3227
Bowl, 9″ x 4″

3228
Bowl, 7½″ x 4″

3229
Bowl, 6, 9 or 12″

3229
Candleholder, 3¼″

3236
Wall pocket, 7″

3237
Wall pocket, 8″

3238
Wall pocket, 9″

3239
Server, Leaf, 8″

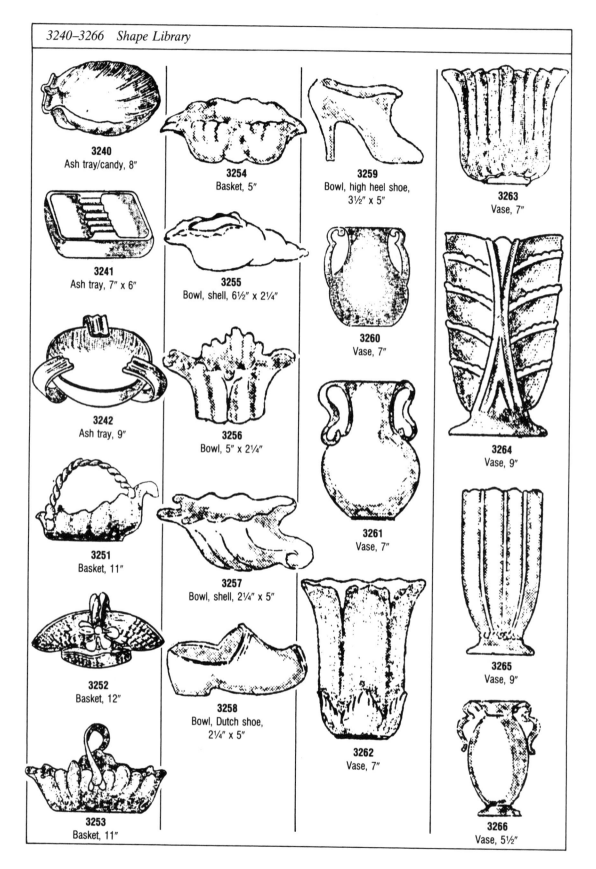

3240
Ash tray/candy, 8″

3241
Ash tray, 7″ x 6″

3242
Ash tray, 9″

3251
Basket, 11″

3252
Basket, 12″

3253
Basket, 11″

3254
Basket, 5″

3255
Bowl, shell, 6½″ x 2¼″

3256
Bowl, 5″ x 2¼″

3257
Bowl, shell, 2¼″ x 5″

3258
Bowl, Dutch shoe,
2¼″ x 5″

3259
Bowl, high heel shoe,
3½″ x 5″

3260
Vase, 7″

3261
Vase, 7″

3262
Vase, 7″

3263
Vase, 7″

3264
Vase, 9″

3265
Vase, 9″

3266
Vase, 5½″

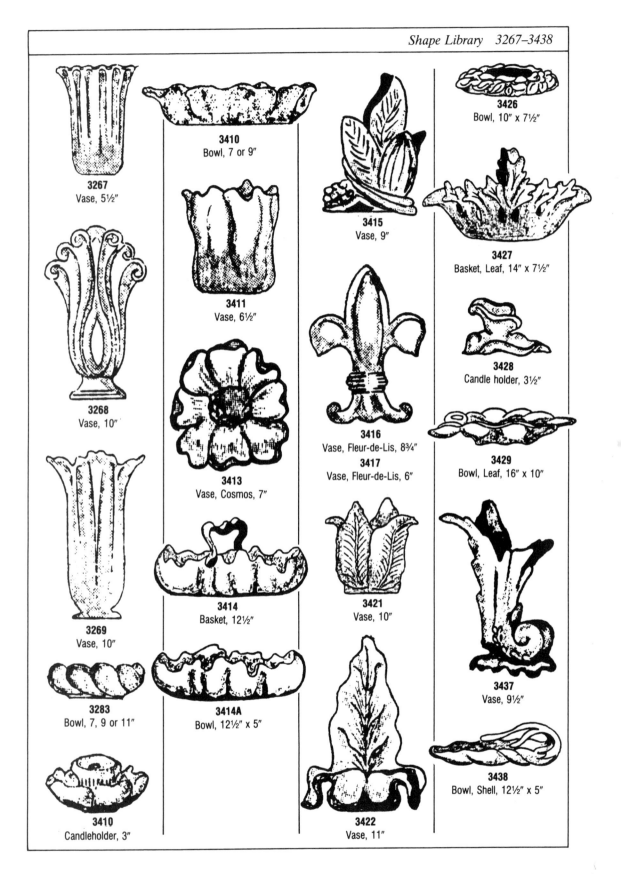

3267
Vase, 5½"

3410
Bowl, 7 or 9"

3415
Vase, 9"

3426
Bowl, 10" x 7½"

3427
Basket, Leaf, 14" x 7½"

3268
Vase, 10"

3411
Vase, 6½"

3416
Vase, Fleur-de-Lis, 8¾"

3417
Vase, Fleur-de-Lis, 6"

3428
Candle holder, 3½"

3429
Bowl, Leaf, 16" x 10"

3413
Vase, Cosmos, 7"

3269
Vase, 10"

3414
Basket, 12½"

3421
Vase, 10"

3437
Vase, 9½"

3283
Bowl, 7, 9 or 11"

3414A
Bowl, 12½" x 5"

3438
Bowl, Shell, 12½" x 5"

3410
Candleholder, 3"

3422
Vase, 11"

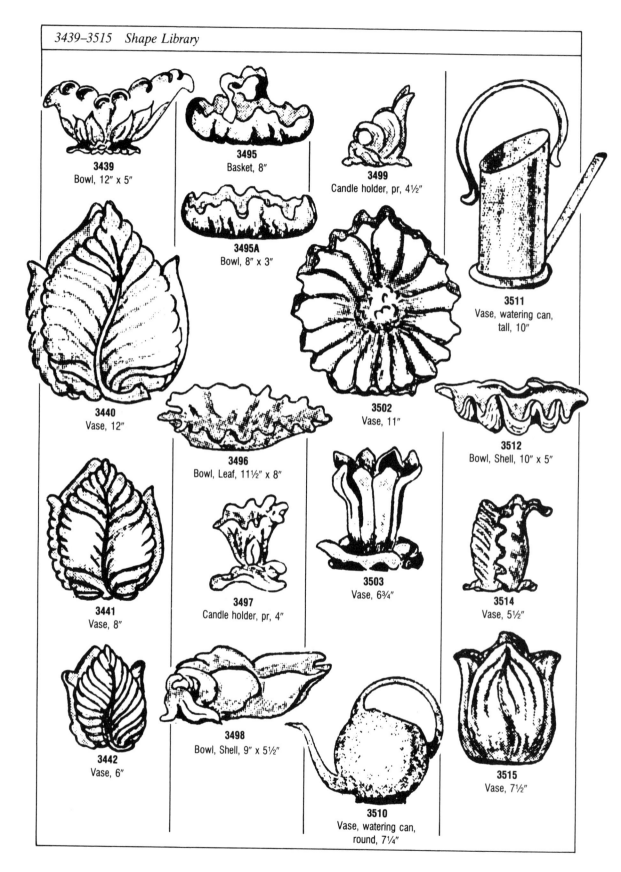

3439
Bowl, 12″ x 5″

3495
Basket, 8″

3495A
Bowl, 8″ x 3″

3499
Candle holder, pr, 4½″

3511
Vase, watering can,
tall, 10″

3440
Vase, 12″

3502
Vase, 11″

3496
Bowl, Leaf, 11½″ x 8″

3512
Bowl, Shell, 10″ x 5″

3441
Vase, 8″

3497
Candle holder, pr, 4″

3503
Vase, 6¾″

3514
Vase, 5½″

3442
Vase, 6″

3498
Bowl, Shell, 9″ x 5½″

3515
Vase, 7½″

3510
Vase, watering can,
round, 7¼″

144

3517
Bowl, 2½″ x 5½″

3520
Ash tray, Leaf, 4½″ x 4″

3520/20
Cigarette Box, 4″ x 3½″

3521
Ash tray, Leaf, 5½″ x 4″

3520/21
Cigarette Box, 4″ x 3½″

3522
Ash tray, Shell, 5″ x 4½″

3523
Ash tray, Leaf, 6¼″ x 4″

3524
Ash tray, Leaf, 5¼″ x 4¼″

3525
Ash tray, Leaf, 5½″ x 4″

3526
Ash tray, Flower, 5½″ x 5″

3527
Ash tray, Leaf, 4¼″ x 3″

3528
Ash tray, Leaf, 3¼″ x 3″

3529
Ash tray, Leaf, 4″ x 3½″

3530
Ash tray, Oak leaf, 4″ x 2¾″

3531
Ash tray, Leaf, 3½″ square

3532
Ash tray, Leaf, 5¾″ x 4½″

3535
Bowl, Leaf, 16″ x 13″

3536
Bowl, Leaf, 18″ x 12½″

3537
Bowl, Leaf, 18″ x 11″

3538
Bowl, Oak Leaf, 17″ x 13″

3539
Bowl, Leaf, 12″ x 9″

3540
Bowl, Leaf, 13″ x 7¾″

3541
Bowl, Leaf, 12¾″ x 7½″

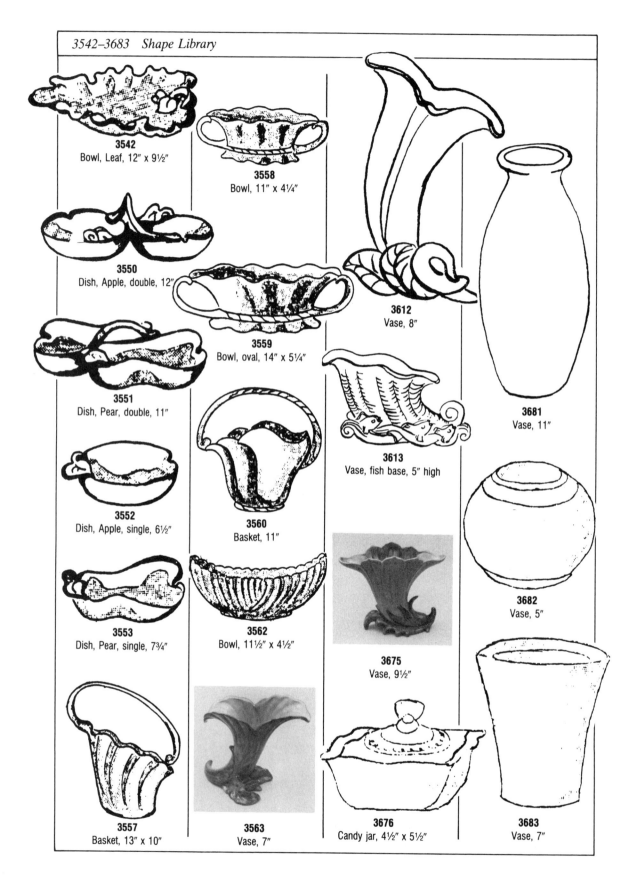

3542
Bowl, Leaf, 12″ x 9½″

3558
Bowl, 11″ x 4¼″

3550
Dish, Apple, double, 12″

3551
Dish, Pear, double, 11″

3559
Bowl, oval, 14″ x 5¼″

3552
Dish, Apple, single, 6½″

3560
Basket, 11″

3553
Dish, Pear, single, 7¾″

3562
Bowl, 11½″ x 4½″

3557
Basket, 13″ x 10″

3563
Vase, 7″

3612
Vase, 8″

3613
Vase, fish base, 5″ high

3675
Vase, 9½″

3676
Candy jar, 4½″ x 5½″

3681
Vase, 11″

3682
Vase, 5″

3683
Vase, 7″

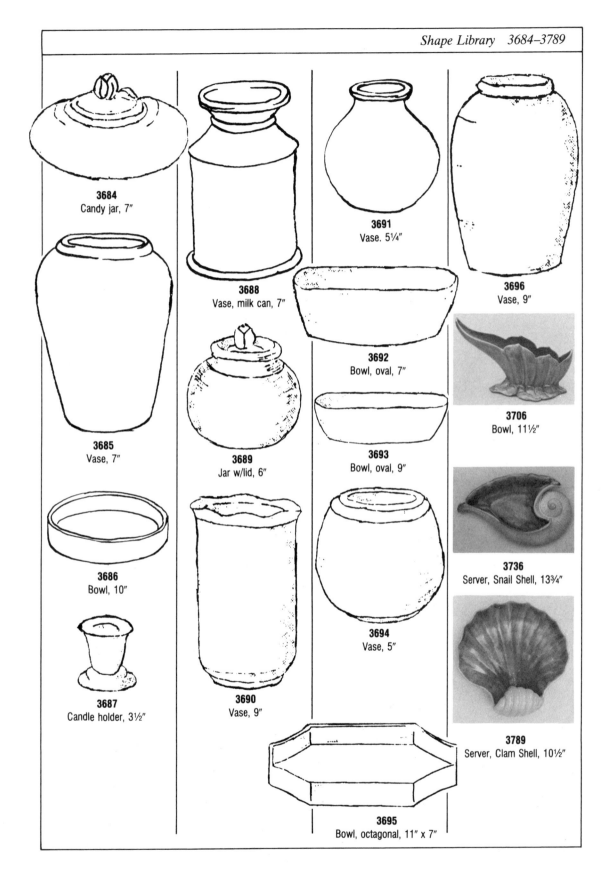

3684
Candy jar, 7″

3685
Vase, 7″

3686
Bowl, 10″

3687
Candle holder, 3½″

3688
Vase, milk can, 7″

3689
Jar w/lid, 6″

3690
Vase, 9″

3691
Vase. 5¼″

3692
Bowl, oval, 7″

3693
Bowl, oval, 9″

3694
Vase, 5″

3695
Bowl, octagonal, 11″ x 7″

3696
Vase, 9″

3706
Bowl, 11½″

3736
Server, Snail Shell, 13¾″

3789
Server, Clam Shell, 10½″

147

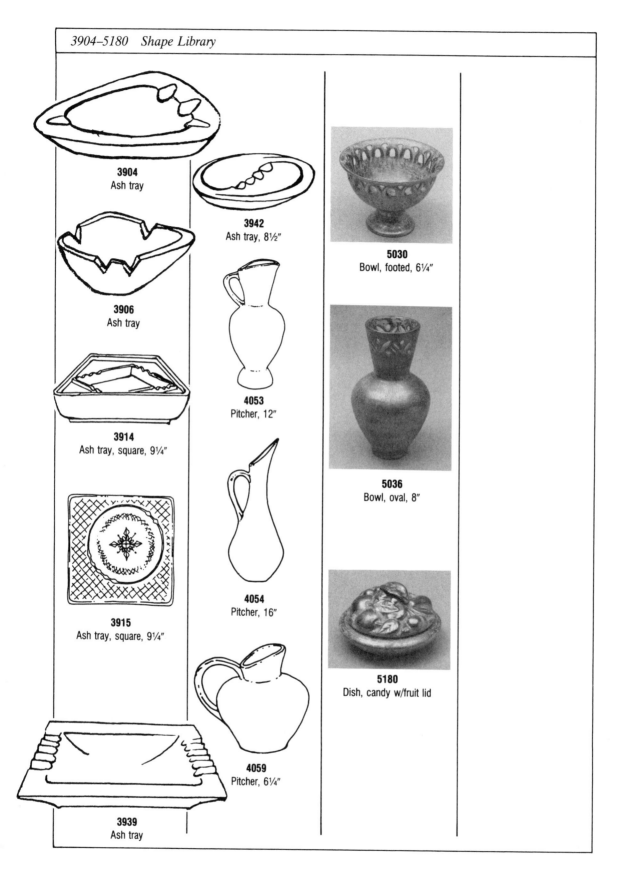

3904
Ash tray

3942
Ash tray, 8½″

3906
Ash tray

3914
Ash tray, square, 9¼″

3915
Ash tray, square, 9¼″

4053
Pitcher, 12″

4054
Pitcher, 16″

4059
Pitcher, 6¼″

3939
Ash tray

5030
Bowl, footed, 6¼″

5036
Bowl, oval, 8″

5180
Dish, candy w/fruit lid

Index